Max O'Rell

John Bull & Co.

The great colonial branches of the firm, Canada, Australia, New Zealand and South Africa

Max O'Rell

John Bull & Co.
The great colonial branches of the firm, Canada, Australia, New Zealand and South Africa

ISBN/EAN: 9783744754729

Printed in Europe, USA, Canada, Australia, Japan

Cover: Foto ©Suzi / pixelio.de

More available books at **www.hansebooks.com**

JOHN BULL & CO.

THE AUTHOR WITH A GOLD CONVOY ON THE WAY TO DURBAN.
(From a Photograph taken by H. S. Ellerbeck, Natal.)

JOHN BULL & CO.

THE GREAT COLONIAL BRANCHES OF THE FIRM:
CANADA, AUSTRALIA, NEW ZEALAND
AND SOUTH AFRICA

BY

MAX O'RELL

AUTHOR OF "JOHN BULL AND HIS ISLAND," "JONATHAN AND HIS CONTINENT,"
"A FRENCHMAN IN AMERICA," ETC., ETC.

NEW YORK
CHARLES L. WEBSTER & COMPANY
1894

COPYRIGHT, 1894,
BY BAINBRIDGE COLBY.
[*All rights reserved.*]

PRESS OF
JENKINS & McCOWAN,
NEW YORK.

TO
MY TRAVELING COMPANIONS
AROUND THE WORLD,

MY WIFE
AND
MY DAUGHTER.

CONTENTS.

	PAGE
AN INTRODUCTORY REMINDER	11

CHAPTER I
France, the First Country of the World—Foreigners, and what is Understood by the Term—Britishers—Englishmen at Home and Germans Abroad—Branch Establishments of John Bull & Co. 15

CHAPTER II
French Canada—Quebec—A Bit of France Buried in the Snow—The French Canadians are the French of the Seventeenth Century—Puritan Catholicism—The Frozen St. Lawrence—Montreal—Canadian Sports—I Meet Tartarin . . 22

CHAPTER III
Ottawa—Toronto—The Canadian Women—Winnipeg and St. Boniface, or England and France, Ten Minutes' Walk from Each Other—The Political Parties of Canada. . . 29

CHAPTER IV
Flying Through the Far West—The Prairies—Colorado—Denver—The Rockies—Salt Lake City—The Mormons—The Desert—The Sierras—The Plains of California—San Francisco—China Town—Impressions Confirmed—A Branch of the Firm John Bull & Co. Started in Business for Itself . 33

CHAPTER V
The Pacific Ocean—The Sandwich Islands—Honolulu—The Southern Cross—What a Swindle !—The Samoan Islands—Apia—Mr. Robert Louis Stevenson—Auckland—Arrival of the Philistines 40

CHAPTER VI
Sydney—I have seen the Harbor—The Australia Hotel—The French in Sydney—The Town—The Parks—Cupid in the Open Air—Little Clandestine Visits to the South Head—" Engaged " — Melbourne—Activity — All Scottish — The Holy Tartufes—Adelaide—Brisbane—Ballarat—Bendigo—Geelong 51

CONTENTS.

CHAPTER VII

People of Society, People in Society, and "Society" People—The "Sets"—Society Papers—" Miss D. Looked Thrillingly Lovely in Electric Blue"—The Australian Women are Beautiful—Imitation of the Old World—A Tasmanian Snob—Darling Point, Pott's Point, and Sore Point—A Melbourne Journalist on His Townspeople 71

CHAPTER VIII

Hospitality in the Colonies—Different People at Home and Abroad—Extreme Courtesy of the Australian—Childishness—Visit to the Four Everlasting Buildings of the Colonial Towns—Impressions—Wild Expenditure—Give Us a Prison—" Who is Bismarck?"—" Don't know "—In the Olden Time 79

CHAPTER IX

Colonial "Cheek"—Mutual Admiration Society—An Inquisitive Colonial—A Verbatim Conversation—An Amiable Landlord—Modest Politicians—Advice to England by an Australian Minister—Provincialisms—Napier—Opinions on Madame Sarah Bernhardt—Mr. H. M. Stanley and the Municipal Councilor—The Czar had Better Behave Himself—I Introduce Sophocles to the Colonies and Serve Corneille a Bad Turn—An Invitation Accepted with a Vengeance . . 87

CHAPTER X

The Curse of the Colonies—A Perfect Gentleman—A Town Full of Animation—A Drunkard Begs me to give the Audience a Lecture on Waterloo—A Jolly Fellow—Pater Familias on the Spree—An Ingenious Drunkard—Great Feats—Taverns and Teetotalers—Why there are no Cafés in the Colonies—A Philosopher—Why a Young English Girl could not get Engaged 101

CHAPTER XI

Types—Caprices of Nature—Men and Women—Precocious Children—Prehistoric Dress—Timidity of the Women—I Shock some Tasmanian Ladies—Anglo-Saxon Contrasts . . 116

CHAPTER XII

The Bush—The Eucalyptus—The Climate—Description of the Bush and its Inhabitants—The Concert of the Bush—The Tragedians and the Clowns of the Company—The Kangaroo—The Workers and the Idlers of the Bush—Beggars on Horseback 122

CONTENTS.

CHAPTER XIII

The Most Piquant Thing in Australia—Aspect of the Small Towns—Each takes his Pleasure where he Finds it—Australian Life—Tea, always Tea—Whiskey or Water—Favorite Occupation—Seven Meals a Day—Squatters . . 131

CHAPTER XIV

The Australian Natives—The Last Tasmanian is in the Museum —A Broken-down King Accepts my Penny—Diana Pays me a Visit—The Trackers—The Queensland Aborigines—The Boomerang—Curious Rites—The Ladies Refuse to Wash for the Bachelors 142

CHAPTER XV

Politics and Politicians—The Price of Liberty—The Legislative Chambers—Governors—Comparisons between American and British Institutions—The Politician and the Order of St. Michael and St. George—An Eloquent Candidate—The Honorables—Colonial Peerage—Sir Henry Parkes—A Word to Her Majesty Queen Victoria 148

CHAPTER XVI

The Resources of Australia—The Mines—2,500 Per Cent. Dividends—Wool—Viticulture—The Wealth of Australia Compared to the Wealth of Most Other Countries—Why France is Richer than Other Nations 156

CHAPTER XVII

The Workman Sovereign Master of Australia—His Character— The Artist and the Bungler—A Sham Democrat—Government by and for the Workingman—Public Orators—Stories of Workmen—End of the Tragic Story of a Russian Traveler 162

CHAPTER XVIII

The Religions of the Colonies—The Catholic Church and Its Work—The Baptists and the Sweet Shops—Good News for the Little Ones—A Presbyterian Landlady in Difficulties—I Give a Presbyterian Minister His Deserts—Christian Association of Good Young Men—The Big Drum, or the Church at the Fair—Pious Bankers—An Edifying Prayer . . 170

CHAPTER XIX

The Australian Newspapers—The Large Dailies—Weekly Editions—The "Australasian"—The Comic Papers—The Society Papers—The "Bulletin" 184

CONTENTS.

CHAPTER XX

Amusements at the Antipodes—The Australian Gayer than the Englishman — Melbourne — Lord Hopetoun — The Racing Craze—The Melbourne Cup—Flemington Compared with Longchamps and Epsom 188

CHAPTER XXI

The Drama in the Colonies—Madame Sarah Bernhardt in Australia—Anglo-Saxon Theatres Compared with Theatres in Paris—Variety Shows—The Purveyor of Intellectual Pleasures—An Important Actor—The Theatre in Small Towns 195

CHAPTER XXII

Railroads in the Colonies—You Set Out but You Do Not Arrive—A Woman in a Hurry—Mixed Trains—First Class Travelers—Curious Traveling Companions 202

CHAPTER XXIII

Spirit of Nationality and Independence—Local Patriotism—Every Man for himself and the Colonies for the Colonials . 206

CHAPTER XXIV

Tasmania—The Country—The Inhabitants of Other Days and the Inhabitants of the Present Day—Visit to the Depots—Survivors of the "Ancien Régime"—A Tough old Scotchwoman—A Touching Scene—Launceston and Hobart . 210

CHAPTER XXV

New Zealand—Norway and Switzerland at the Antipodes—The Point of the Earth's Surface that is Farthest from Paris—No Snakes, but a Great Many Scots—The Small Towns—A Curious Inscription 219

CHAPTER XXVI

The Maoris—Types—Tattooing—Ways and Customs—Native Chivalry—The Legends of the Country—Sir George Grey—Lucky Landlords—The "Haka"—The Beautiful Victoria—Maori Villages—New Zealand the Prettiest Country in the World 227

CHAPTER XXVII

From Melbourne to the Cape of Good Hope—The "Australasian"—Sunday on Board Ship—Conversions—Death of a Poor Mother—Ceremony—Table Bay—Arrival at Cape Town . 240

CONTENTS.

CHAPTER XXVIII

Anglo-Dutch—John Bull, Charged with the Care of the Cape for the Prince of Orange, Keeps it for Himself—Mixture of Races—Cape Town—The Town and its Environs—Paarl—The Huguenots — Stellenbosch — Happy Folk — Drapers' Assistants—Independence a Characteristic Feature of South Africans 245

CHAPTER XXIX

The Dutch Puritans—"The Doppers"—A Case of Conscience—The Afrikander-Bond — Its Relations with John Bull—Tickets at Reduced Price—John Bull lies Low—"God Save the Queen" in the South African Republic . . . 253

CHAPTER XXX

Mr. Rhodes, Premier of Cape Colony—The Man—His Work—His Aim 257

CHAPTER XXXI

South African Towns—The Hotels—The Usefulness of the Moon—Kaffirland — Kimberley — The Diamond Mines—The De Beers Company—A Week's Find—Life in the "Compounds"—A Disagreeable Week before going to buy Wives . 260

CHAPTER XXXII

The Country—The "Veld"—The Plateaus—The Climate—The South African Animals—The Ant-hills—The South Coast—Natal—Durban, the Prettiest Town in South Africa—Zulus and Coolies 271

CHAPTER XXXIII

The Natives of South Africa—First Disappointment—Natives in a Natural State — Scenes of Savage Life—The Kraal—Customs—The Women—Types—Among the Kaffirs and the Zulus—Zulus in "Undress"—I buy a Lady's Costume, and Carry it off in my Pocket—What Strange Places Virtue Hides in—The Missionaries gone to the Wrong Place . 279

CHAPTER XXXIV

The Orange Free State—The Transvaal—A Page or Two of History—The Boers at Home—Manners and Customs—The Boers and the Locusts—The Boers will have to "Mend or End"—Bloemfontein, Pretoria, and Johannesburg . . 292

CHAPTER XXXV

Johannesburg, the Gold City—The Boers again—The Future of the Transvaal—Miraculous Development of Johannesburg—Strange Society—Stranger Wives and Husbands—Aristocracy in Low Water—The Captain and the Magistrate . 300

CHAPTER XXXVI

"Oom" Paul, President of the Transvaal—John Bull's Redoubtable Adversary—A Short Interview with this Interesting Personage—A Picturesque Meeting between two Diplomats 307

CHAPTER XXXVII

The Success of the Firm, John Bull & Co. — The Explanation—The Freest Countries of the World—Illustrations to Prove it—The Future of the British Empire—Reflections of a Sour Critic—Advice to Young Men—And Now Let Us Go Back and Look on an Old Wall Covered with Ivy . . . 313

AN INTRODUCTORY REMINDER.

An Englishman was one day swaggering before a Frenchman about the immensity of the British Empire, and he concluded his remarks by saying, "Please to remember, my dear sir, that the sun never sets on the possessions of the English." "I am not surprised at that," replied the good Frenchman; "the sun is obliged to always keep an eye on the rascals."

Here are the details of that British Empire which prevents the sun from enjoying a few hours' rest every night. I borrow them, bringing them up to date, from *John Bull and his Island*, of which volume this is the companion and supplement.

"John Bull's estate, which he quietly adds a little piece to day by day, consists of the British Isles, to which he has given the rather queer name of *United Kingdom*, to make you believe that Pat is fond of him; the Channel Islands; the fortress of Gibraltar, which enables him to pass comfortably through the narrowest of straits; and the islands of Malta and Cyprus, that serve him as advanced sentinels in the Mediterranean. He has not Constantinople—which is to be regretted.

If ever he should get it, he would be satisfied with his slice of Europe.

"In Egypt he is not quite at home yet. He took great care not to invent the Suez Canal. On the contrary, he moved heaven and earth to try and prevent its being made, and he called M. Ferdinand de Lesseps, at the time he conceived the idea, 'a dangerous lunatic.' To-day he has £4,000,000 of public money invested in the concern, and I have no doubt that now, as he receives his dividends, he takes quite a different view of that great undertaking.

"From Aden, on the other side of the Indian Ocean, he can quietly contemplate the finest jewel in his crown, the Indian Empire—an empire of two hundred and eighty-five millions of people, ruled by princes literally covered with gold and precious stones, who black his boots and look happy.

"On the West Coast of Africa he possesses Sierra Leone, Gambia, the Gold Coast, Lagos, Ascension, St. Helena, where he kept in chains the greatest soldier and the most formidable monarch of modern times. In the East, the Island of Mauritius belongs to him. In the South, he has the Cape of Good Hope, Natal, and he *protects* Zululand, Pondoland, Basutoland, Nyassaland, Bechuanaland, Mashonaland, Matabeleland, and a few other little *lands* about there.

"In America he does not possess quite as much as he used to, but he says he does not want it. He still reckons among his possessions there, Canada, Newfoundland, Bermuda, the West Indies, Jamaica, part of Honduras, the Island of Trinidad, English Guiana, Falkland, etc.

"Correctly speaking, Oceanica belongs to him entirely. New Zealand is twice as large as England, and Australia alone covers an area equal to that of almost the whole of Europe.

"'But what shall it profit a man if he gain the whole world and lose his own soul?' says Scripture. This is just what John Bull thought, and so, in the other world, he has knocked down to himself the kingdom of heaven, in his eyes as incontestably a British possession as India, Canada, or Australia."

With the exception of a few omissions, more or less important, such are the assets of the firm, *John Bull & Co.*

JOHN BULL & CO.

CHAPTER I.

France the First Country of the World—Foreigners, and what is Understood by the Term—Britishers—Englishmen at Home and Germans Abroad—Branch Establishments of John Bull & Co.

FRANCE is the foremost country of the world. This is a fact which it were puerile to seek to prove, seeing that the French admit it themselves.

Happy and content in their own country, which is able to support them, the French, of all the nations of the world, are the people who least bother their heads about what is happening outside it: in fact, the masses of the people are in crass ignorance about the rest of the planet.

The Englishman somewhat despises foreigners; the Swiss loves them as the sportsman loves game; the German looks upon them as heaven-sent blessings that permit him to earn a peaceful living far from his fatherland, now turned into a huge garrison. The Frenchman has quite a different feeling toward foreigners: he does not dislike, nor does he despise them; he pities them, and thinks them vastly amusing. The Frenchman even believes in his heart that foreigners were created and sent into the world to minister to his diversion. He looks upon the Belgian as a dear, good simpleton, the Italian as a noisy nobody, the German as a heavy, pompous pedant; he thinks the Americans mad and the English eccentric and grotesque. And he goes on his way delighted.

I have seen French people laugh side-splittingly when I told them that the English drink champagne with their dinner and claret at dessert.

To be sure, my own way of looking at these things is very much the same. How should it be otherwise? After all, a Frenchman is a Frenchman to the end of the chapter.

However, eight years of constant traveling about the world must have rubbed off some of my angles in the way of French provincialism, and I believe myself to have become so far cosmopolitan that the reader may accept as pretty impartial the impressions (I say *impressions* and not *opinions*) contained in this little volume.

Of one thing, at all events, I am firmly convinced, and that is that one nation is not better nor worse than another; each one is different from the others, that is all. This is a deep conviction forced upon one by travel.

To a great many people, the word *foreigner* signifies a droll creature, a kind of savage. In the eyes of a traveler, a foreigner is a worthy man who is as good as himself, and who belongs to a nation which has as many good qualities as the one that he himself hails from. After all, no one is born a foreigner: we all belong somewhere, do we not?

I remember an American who opened a conversation with me by launching at me, as a preliminary, the following question:

" Foreigner, ain't you? "

" I shall be," I replied, " when I set foot in your country."

We were on board the steamer between Liverpool and New York.

If everyone traveled much, the peace of the world would be secure.

" Traveling," said Madam de Staël, " is a sad pleasure." I think it is a most interesting occupation; besides, is it not, up to now, the only way that has been invented for seeing and knowing the world? Man interests me everywhere, whether he be white or black, civilized or savage, and that is why I travel.

But in this volume the subject for treatment is not the world in general, but that British world of which England itself gives but a faint idea. To see the Englishman—the Britisher, rather—in all his glory, you must look at him in those lands where he has elbow-room, where nothing trammels him and where he has been allowed to freely develop his characteristic traits. It was with this object in view that I set out two years ago to visit him in all imaginable climates, from forty below zero to a hundred and ten above (perfect Turkish baths); that I pushed into the far corners of Canada and the United States; visited the islands of the Pacific, Australia, Tasmania, New Zealand, from north to south, from east to west; traveled all over South Africa, Cape Colony, Natal, the now independent republics of the Transvaal and the Orange Free State; in a word, all those worlds which English energy has raised, as if by enchantment, in the most distant oceans.

Another conviction that I have acquired in traveling

is that nations are like individuals : when they succeed at something, it is because they possess qualities which explain their success. And I hope the reader, when he closes these pages, will be able to explain to himself how the English have succeeded in founding the British Empire.

India I have kept for another voyage.

India is not a colony in the proper sense of the word ; it is a possession, an asset of the firm, John Bull & Co., whereas the Colonies which I visited are branches of the said firm. The difference is very distinct.

In India is to be seen John Bull Pacha, a *grand seigneur*, followed by gaily robed servitors who do profound obeisance to him. It is the master in the midst of a subjected people. In the Colonies the conquered races have been suppressed. In Canada you see John Bull quite at home, busy, fat and flourishing, a pink tip to his nose, and his head snug in a fur cap : it is John Bull in a ball. It is the seal. In Australia you see him long and lean, *nonchalant*, happy-go-lucky, his face sunburned, his head crowned with a wide-brimmed light felt hat, walking with slow tread, his arms pendant, his legs out of all proportion. It is John Bull drawn out. It is the kangaroo.

But it is John Bull still, John Bull Junior, eating his morning porridge, and living just as if he were still in his old island, eating his roast beef and plum pudding, and washing it down with tea or whiskey. He is hardly changed at all.

Two full years without a break, what a voyage ! Two years without speaking, and almost without hearing, anything but English! No French to be heard anywhere except in Canada—what a humiliation for a fellow-countryman of Jacques Cartier! However, something that cheered me greatly was that everywhere I went I found Germans blacking boots and waiting at table. I neither speak nor understand German, and am foolish enough to boast of it; but this has caused me no inconvenience of any kind. The Germans speak English and even frequently forget their own tongue. This is very sensible of them, for it is far easier to learn any other language than to try to remember German. And that is why the Germans of New York, Chicago, Sydney, Adelaide, and the Cape speak, think, believe, and pray with the English.

I one day asked a distinguished English writer, who had been around the world several times, whether he intended to publish his impressions of Australia.

"My dear fellow," he replied, "the inhabitants of the Colonies are so kind, so hospitable, so proud of their country! How on earth can I write a book and tell them how bored I was all the time I was there?"

It is a fact that no one can expect to find the country that has a future as interesting as the one that has a past. My English *confrère* was not only a writer, he was an artist, and young countries seldom contain the wherewith to satisfy artistic tastes. On the other hand, if you have any sympathy with your subject, if human nature interests you, if you are curious to learn how nations have been born, and how national character is developed, is there not in the Colonies, just as in the United States, a vast field of observation to explore?

Sixty years ago England used to send her convicts to

Australia, as we French still send ours to New Caledonia. At the present time Australia has towns as important and as populous as Marseilles and Liverpool.

Will it not interest us to have a look at John Bull disguised as an Australian, swearing by Australia, and ready to send the English about their business if ever they should take it upon them to meddle too much with his affairs? Will it not be interesting to watch the evolution of all the eccentricities of the English character?

If the English writer in question found his sojourn in Australia tiresome, I found mine very entertaining. It is true that I missed seeing many picturesque scenes; but that was not my fault. I was in the hands of an impresario,* who constantly reminded me, when I asked him to take me to see some renowned beautiful place in the neighborhood, that he was not a tourist agent, but only a lecture manager; and he understood his business so well that it would have been ungrateful on my part to utter a murmur. My manager appeared to have no taste for scenery, and the finest prospect that could be offered to his gaze was a hall crowded with people who had come to hear me talk.

If I did not see all the country, I believe I saw all the people. This is the essential point in the case of studies which, light as they may be, are studies of character.

Let us, then, study the English in all those countries that are to be seen marked in red on the maps of the

---

* Between September 21, 1891, and August 21, 1893, I gave 446 public lectures in the United States, Canada, Australia and New Zealand and South Africa, under the direction of Major Pond in America, and of Mr. Robert S. Smythe in the Colonies.

world published in England—countries that John Bull has acquired at the cost of very little blood and a good deal of whiskey, always converting the natives to Christianity and their territory to his own uses.

CHAPTER II.

French Canada*—Quebec—A Bit of France Buried in the Snow—The French Canadians are the French of the Seventeenth Century—Puritan Catholicism—The Frozen St. Lawrence—Montreal—Canadian Sports—I Meet Tartarin.

IF you are in a hurry to reach San Francisco, book your seat by the New York Central Railway, but make a short halt at the Falls of Niagara, for the world has nothing grander to offer to your sight. When you have well feasted your eyes and drunk in the wonders around you, take the next train, and for two days and a half travel incessantly: get over the ground as fast as you can, and you may as well lower the blinds to spare yourself the monotony of the interminable prairies. Read, eat, smoke, and sleep, if you can. When you get within twenty or thirty miles of Denver, lift the blinds again and look about you, for the Rocky Mountains are in sight. From Denver to San Francisco do not miss a single detail of the landscape; a series of enchantments awaits you and will unfold itself, hour after hour, as the train flies along the rails. If, however, you are not in a hurry, pay a visit to Canada, French Canada especially, for it is the quaintest and perhaps the most interesting part of the great Western Continent.

In America, John Bull does not possess quite as much as he used to; but he says he does not want it. He is

* On this journey I only spent a few days in Canada. In a former volume I wrote some impressions of that country.

a philosopher. He even goes so far as to congratulate his cousin Jonathan on having made himself master in his own house, and certain wise people in Britain assert that it was predicted in the Holy Scriptures that the House of Israel should one day be divided, and that an important remnant of it would declare its independence. By the House of Israel, or the chosen people of God, must be understood the British nation; the remnant is America. It is all as plain as A B C.

Canada still belongs to England, and it is a very pretty dependency, with a superficial area almost equal to that of the United States.

I know nothing more picturesque than the scenery between New York and Albany along the Hudson River in autumn, when America has wrapped herself in her mantle of scarlet and gold, and the clear blue sky is reflected in the dancing waves of the noble Hudson.

From Albany, pass into Maine and New England, across immense pine forests, and later the White Mountains, dominated by Mount Washington. Passes, precipices, waterfalls, beautify the landscape, and Switzerland has nothing wilder or more picturesque to offer. From there push on into Canada, and let your first halt be at Quebec, on the confluence of the St. Lawrence and the St. Charles rivers.

When I visited Quebec the ice of winter was breaking up, and the rivers were full of small icebergs, which made the crossing from the train at Pont Levis quite an exciting voyage. The skipper of the ferry-boat waited and watched until a comparatively clear passage seemed possible, and at last, with many twistings and dodgings and bumps, the boat reached the Quebec quay. The people speak of this annual break-up of winter as "the flood," and when the melted snow comes down from the upper town, a house in the lower part of Quebec must be anything but a desirable residence. In many streets the roadway had been raised eight or ten feet by the snows which had been cleared from the pavements after each fall and heaped up in the road.

QUEBEC.

Along this elevated way the sleighs ran above the level of the pedestrian's head.

The grandeur of the mighty cliff, crowned with the citadel, charms your gaze, and a stroll through the city will make you believe you have strayed into some old Breton town, the sing-song intonation in the people's speech, the sign-boards over the doors, *Au Bon St. Jo-*

seph, À Notre Dame des Douleurs, Au Petit Agneau sans Tache, the Breton and Norman names of the shopkeepers, the *Hue-là* of the carters urging on their horses, all help to complete the illusion.

Only a Norman or a Breton could feel the pleasure and emotion that I felt at seeing these children of old France in Quebec, speaking and thinking as the French spoke and thought in Louis XIV.'s time. Their language has remained the old Norman dialect of the *langue d'oïl*, such as the peasants of lower Normandy speak it to-day, innocent of diphthongs. *Si t'as sef, ch ben va bère un coup.* You will hear *core* for *encore*, *des foués* for *quelquefois*, *à cette heure* for *maintenant*. Add to this the influence of the English language, and you have the explanation of such expressions as the following: *être particulier* for *faire attention*, *résigner* for *donner sa démission*, *lecturer* for *faire des conférences*, *crosser* for *traverser*, *laisser* for *quitter*. The preterite tense is frequently employed instead of the past indefinite. Thus you may read in a newspaper: *Le Gouverneur laissa Québec ce matin* for *le Gouverneur a quitté Québec ce matin.*

The Catholicism of the French Canadians is not the genial and cheerful religion of these days, but the Catholicism which in France, two hundred years ago, had to compete with Calvinism, and was austere, sombre, harsh, tyrannical and almost puritanical, and which to-day in Canada forbids round dances and frowns on many innocent pleasures.

Education is directed by the priests, who, in return for this concession on the part of John Bull, stimulate none but feelings of loyalty to the English Crown. This is part of the excellent plan adopted by the English in governing their Colonies all over the world. One result of the wise laxity of rule is that the French Canadians take little part in politics. They are content to belong to England, because it means liberty, and assures them the enjoyment of their earnings. The French Canadians are hard-working and thrifty; they marry very young, and have large families; in fact, they increase almost as rapidly as the population of the British Isles; and families of twelve, fifteen, even twenty children are not uncommon. Few of the sons go away from home, and the province of Quebec bids fair to be soon as French as the city itself.

What brightness, what briskness there is in the winter climate of Canada! and how astonishingly little one feels the cold under that blue and sunny sky, though the thermometer may mark forty degrees below zero! I was told that many men do not wear an overcoat during their first winter in Canada, except when driving. The air is so dry and full of electricity that everything metallic which you touch brings an electric spark from your finger-nails. I several times lit the gas by means of this spark. When you drive, it is in open sleighs. There are few covered ones. But you are muffled in furs to the very eyes, and glow with warmth as the sleigh goes merrily over the frozen snow with tinkling bells. In Montreal, and other gay cities of Canada, winter is full of delights. Skating, sleighing, tobogganing and snow-shoeing parties are the order of the day, and, I may add, night, for the latter generally take place by moonlight. On my arrival at Montreal, about six hours' journey from Quebec, I was straightway taken to see some racing on the St. Lawrence. Not boat-races, but horse-races. The ice on the river is about three feet thick in winter, and tram-rails are laid across for a service of cars. A novel and astonishing sight it was to me to see the horses drawing those heavy loads over the ice, as if it had been a macadamized road. Then there are the ice-boats, which skim over

MONTREAL. FROM MOUNT ROYAL PARK.

the ice at such breathless speed that to remain on their decks at all you have to lie down and hold on.

Montreal is the town of sports and gaiety *par excellence;* it is the home of the ice-palace. Many and merry are the *fêtes* held within those glittering walls built of blocks of ice cemented with water. And where else can such toboggan rides be had as the giant slope of Mount Royal provides?

During my stay in Montreal and Quebec, I often met a Frenchman, a good Parisian, a picture of health and happiness, a charming talker, full of life, happy to be alive, and getting amusement out of everything he came across; a little bit Gascon, it is true, but so little; a Tartarin of good society.

The day I left Montreal I met him in the hall of the Windsor Hotel, muffled up in a white woolen hooded tunic, with a red sash around the waist, and on his head a woolen cap, with its tassel jauntily hanging on his shoulder. The costume was completed by immense thick stockings and knickerbockers, and in his hand he carried snow-shoes and an alpenstock—the regular snow-shoeing get-up.

"Aha!" said I; "you are off on an expedition over the snow?"

"Not I," he replied; and his good, open face beamed with fun. "I am going to get photographed.'

Not all the Tarasconnais come from Tarascon.

CHAPTER III.

Ottawa—Toronto—The Canadian Women—Winnipeg and St. Boniface, or England and France Ten Minutes' Walk From Each Other—The Political Parties of Canada.

OTTAWA, three hours by rail from Montreal, is the capital of the Dominion. Like Washington, in the United States, the city is entirely consecrated to politics, and you must not look for anything else in it. However, when you arrive in Ottawa, do not fail to halt a little on the bridge over the river, for you will see a picture worthy of your attention; to right of you the falls and rapids; to left, high against the sky, and standing on an almost perpendicular rock, the Houses of Parliament, a group of superb buildings in stone. It was my good fortune to see it, for the first time, standing out clearly between a brilliant blue sky and a sweep of pure white snow. Inside, the Houses of Parliament are spacious and well appointed: the members are in clover. The library is a very valuable one, and the disposition of the rooms has been admirably thought out and carried out.

As you advance toward the west, in Canada, the towns begin to look more American and the people more English; the web of telegraph and telephone wires overhead grows thicker; the complexion of the women grows more rosy, and, instead of picturesque winding streets, you once more have the parallelograms and rectangular blocks of masonry that came in with tram-rails.

Toronto, built in blocks, with wide streets and houses plastered with flaring advertisements, is very American-looking. But penetrate into the suburbs, and the scene changes: you are reminded of the presence of the English, for most of the pretty villas are set in gardens, and a private garden is a thing rarely seen near American towns. There are no people who are fonder of flowers or more lavish in the use of them than the Americans, yet the growing of them seems to be entirely left to the professional gardener. I heard various reasons given in explanation of the absence of lawns and flower-beds around suburban houses. One was the extreme cold of the winters, another the extreme heat of the summers, but I came to the conclusion that the chief reason was want of time. I do not know whether the villa gardens of Toronto are very gay with flowers in summer. When I saw them they were thickly buried in snow; but there were the trees and shrubs, and there, utterly un-American-looking, was the fence or the wall which reminds one that an Englishman's house is his castle. The American, having no garden, dispenses with a fence, and his house, though it may be a fine mansion, stands but a few feet back from the roadway, with its front door accessible, in truly republican fashion, to every passer-by.

Toronto swarms with churches and pretty women. I never, in any town, saw quite so many of either.

The Canadian lady is a happy combination of her English and American sisters. She has the physical beauty, the tall, graceful figure, and the fine complexion of the former, allied to the decided bearing, the naturalness, the frank glance, and the piquancy of the latter. If, added to these, one could have the shrewd common sense, and the irresistible charm of the *Parisienne*, the result would be a really ideal woman. The amount of outdoor exercise taken by Canadian women in their winter games and pastimes goes far to explain the beauty of their complexions. The air of Canada is dry, the houses are heated in the same way as American houses, yet these two things, often advanced as the cause of the American belles' pallor, do not prevent the Canadian women from having brilliant complexions.

It was in Toronto that I was given an insight into the system of education adopted by the English Canadians. It is practically the American system; boys and girls, rich and poor, sit side by side on their school benches and receive the same instruction. Among the French Canadians, education, as I have already said, is in the hands of the priest, and the standard of instruction is low.

Besides the cities that I have mentioned, Canada possesses many important towns, such as London, Hamilton, etc. One of the most interesting to visit is Winnipeg, in the northwest. To reach it you have to cross, in summer, a veritable ocean of plants and flowers; in winter, an ocean of ice and snow. It is the prairie in its immensity, lonesome but grandiose. A population of thirty thousand people, energetic and intelligent, is chiefly engaged in the commerce of wood and cereals. The town is flourishing, has many fine buildings and a hotel, the Manitoba, which for comfort and luxury has no equal within a circuit of five hundred miles. Ten minutes from the town, across the river, stands the little village of St. Boniface, founded by the French long before Winnipeg was thought of, and which has remained just what it was. In Canada, you are constantly coming across old France standing still, while bustling England advances, spreads, and multiplies. If you set out from Quebec, and follow the course of the St. Lawrence as far as the Mississippi at New Orleans, you can do two thousand miles without going off the line followed by the early French settlers. The names along the route will sufficiently indicate the origin of the towns: Quebec, Montreal, St. Paul, Detroit, Des Moines, St. Louis, New Orleans.

It seems to me that Canada, on account of its interests and its geographical position, is destined one day to become part of the great American family. But if ever the amalgamation should take place, it will be without the firing of a shot or the spilling of a drop of blood.

At present, the number of Canadians in favor of uniting their country to the States is only about one-fourth of the population. Although there are but two political parties, the Liberals and the Conservatives, wherever the annexation question is discussed there appear to be four camps: people in favor of annexation; a party, largely composed of the best society, preferring the present state of things; another, which advocates federation; and a fourth, which would like to see Canada an independent nation. To the last-named party belong most of the French Canadians. They naturally detest the idea of federation, because it would mean to them political annihilation, and as these people form a large and rapidly increasing portion of the population, I imagine that the scheme of federation is little likely ever to be adopted by Canada.

CHAPTER IV.

Flying through the Far West—The Prairies—Colorado—Denver—The Rockies—Salt Lake City—The Mormons—The Desert—The Sierras—The Plains of California—San Francisco—China Town—Impressions Confirmed—A Branch of the Firm John Bull & Co. Started in Business for Itself.

THE journey from Winnipeg to St. Paul in winter is done on an unbroken plain of ice and snow. To go into raptures over a landscape such as this, one must be born in the States. An American would say, " Yes, sir, everything in this country is on an immense scale." St. Paul and its neighbor, Minneapolis, are towns of two hundred and fifty thousand inhabitants each, situated at a distance of only ten miles from each other. Jealousy alone gives a separate existence to these two towns, which ought to form but one. If St. Paul elected to become part of Minneapolis, Minneapolis would have no objection; if Minneapolis decided to merge its individuality in that of St. Paul, St. Paul would think it quite natural. As to any union by common consent, as well ask Manchester and Liverpool to abide by the decisions of one and the same town council.

Twenty-four hours of railway traveling across a flat country takes you from St. Paul to Omaha, a town of more than a hundred thousand inhabitants. Fifteen hours more and you are at Kansas City. Still the monotonous flatness. However, the country, which is entirely consecrated to agriculture and the raising of cattle, is prosperous and not without a certain interest. One day more and you are in Colorado, and nearing Denver. After the dreary monotony of the prairies, the first glimpse of the grand peaks of the Rockies, standing up soft and blue against the western sky, where a gorgeous sun was setting, was a thing to be remembered. Denver, twenty years ago a mining camp, to-day a flourishing, well-built town of one hundred and fifty thousand inhabitants. Such is America. Omaha, Kansas City, Denver, are so many budding Chicagos.

But time is flying. "All aboard!"

A few hours after leaving Denver you enter the Rocky Mountains by a narrow passage which winds between colossal rocks rising straight into the air. The chain of mountains unfolds itself hour by hour to your astonished eyes as the train rushes on with infinite twistings among the giant hills. The panorama is enchanting. Then the train begins to climb, twisting and recoiling on itself like a caterpillar, till its extremities almost touch and form a circle. You reach a height of ten thousand feet above sea level, and the train steams into Leadville, "the cloud city." (Every American town is a city in American parlance.) Leadville was at one time a busy place with a large population, but the lead mines failed to yield as they had been expected to do, and the town is now a forlorn-looking one, lost in the clouds, and with "Ichabod" writ large all over it. Then you descend toward the fertile valley of the Salt Lake in Utah. The Mormons have been described *ad nauseam*, and there is nothing new to be looked for in their midst; they are ancient history. By a new law of the United States, polygamy is no longer tolerated, and if Artemus Ward were now alive, and about to give one of his delightfully humorous talks there, he could no longer put on the complimentary ticket given to some Mormon to whom he wished to show a politeness, "Admit bearer and one wife." In Salt Lake City you are struck by the cleanliness, the quietness, and the general air of prosperity of the place. The Mormons are meek-voiced and mild-mannered, as one would expect in the descendants of an oppressed sect. Attendants are polite and altogether a great contrast to the same class of persons on the other side of the Rockies. The Mormons continue to believe and call themselves Saints. This is a harmless mania that hurts nobody.

TEMPLE SQUARE, SALT LAKE CITY.

Before getting into California there remains but the

State of Nevada to cross, a sandy, arid land, which forms a curious contrast with the fertile Salt Lake valley and the luxuriant plains of California between which it lies. Some Indians, majestically draped in blankets and with feathers in their hair, a few cowboys with sombreros stuck on the back of the head give a touch of the picturesque to this scene of desolation, a scene almost grandiose in its dreariness. After the sandy desert is traversed, the ground begins to rise once more, nature shows signs of life again, and presently you are in the Sierras, which to my thinking are still more picturesque and much grander than the Rockies. The Rocky Mountains are certainly mountainous and undeniably rocky, but the landscape has not the majesty of the Sierras. The Rocky Mountains are wild and arid; the Sierras are luxuriant with verdure. You are nearing the home of perpetual spring. All is gay and smiling: the blue sky, the slopes of the mountains clothed with gigantic trees, the valleys carpeted with ferns and semi-tropical plants. I have seen no other country so enchanting.

After being so long used to looking on nothing but an expanse of snow or a brown desert, the eyes are fairly dazzled by all this verdure. From the Sierras you descend into the plains of California, the train rushing through this vast garden of magnolias, orange and lemon trees, cacti and rich plants of all kinds, and all the way to San Francisco the feast for the eyes is one of unparalleled loveliness. You are in El Dorado.

I confess that San Francisco itself disappointed me. I scarcely know why, but I had an idea that this town must be quite different from the other large towns of America. Its name had suggested to my mind a place half Spanish, half Mexican, with an individuality of its own. In reality it is but another New York, Chicago, or Cincinnati. Market street, the chief street, differs little from Broadway, New York, Washington street, Boston, or State street, Chicago. Everywhere the same square blocks, the eternal parallelograms, the same gaudy advertisements, the same flaring posters. In the quarter where the rich people have taken up their abode the houses are handsome, but have not the gardens one would expect to see around them. The park is beautiful, and very remarkable as being the result of a clever victory over the mass of fine sand that lay between San Francisco and the sea. This sand, which half blinded the city every time the wind blew in from the ocean, is now bound into a fair lawn by buffalo grass, and is planted over with California's lovely trees and flowers. Near by, that is to say at three-quarters of an hour's drive from the town, are the Seal Rocks, covered with the creatures that give them their name, and a visit to them also means a sight of the grand expanse of the Pacific ocean washing in on an apparently endless beach of smooth yellow sand.

But to see a really fine typical Californian town you must go south, to Los Angeles for instance, which town is a veritable poem.

I had heard a great deal about China Town and had been advised not to leave San Francisco without visiting this Chinese quarter. I expected to find a bit of the Orient in this great western city, but what I did see was a slum, a rubbish heap, fit to turn one sick, a disgrace to a town which, after all, must be directed and governed by respectable people. Thirty or forty thousand Chinese swarm in an atmosphere heavy with rancid grease, tobacco, musk, sandal-wood, and in the midst of gambling hells, opium dens, houses of ill fame, the blinds of which are not even lowered, a vile crowd living by the most shameless vice in most ignoble dirt, and this not in some outlying suburb where it might be convenient to fling the rubbish of the community, but in the very centre of the city.

Heaven be praised, I soon forgot the amazing horrors of the place, but the odor of it long hung about my clothing.

For the third time I had visited the United States, and had now seen them from north to south, from east to west. Now I was going to see still newer worlds, Australia, New Zealand, and South Africa, the Americas of the future.

The impressions formed during the two previous voyages seemed to have taken deeper root, and I felt the greater number of them to be confirmed. A country especially interesting from the feverish activity which, in a century, has developed it, and made of it a shining light to the rest of the world in the matter of practical ideas; a people straining every nerve in the race for dollars, suffering from bile and billions, and who have learned most things except the art of good self-government; unique women, the most intellectual and interesting in the world, whom I can admire all the more because I have not the honor to be the husband of one of them, and therefore have not to pay her dressmakers' bills, nor work by the sweat of my brow to cover her with diamonds.

I had intended in this volume only to speak of the English Colonies. However, I do not think that these few remarks on the United States are out of place here. Was not America once one of the great branch establishments of the firm, John Bull & Co., although she may have since set up in business for herself? And is not this the future that is before several other of those branches?

CHAPTER V.

The Pacific Ocean—The Sandwich Islands—Honolulu—The Southern Cross—What a Swindle !—The Samoan Islands—Apia—Mr. Robert Louis Stevenson—Auckland—Arrival of the Philistines.

THE voyage from San Francisco to Auckland in New Zealand takes just three weeks, and, with the exception of the first two days, which are rendered often disagreeable by a shallow sea easily stirred up, the passage is generally delightful. During nineteen days we found the Pacific Ocean as calm as a lake.

The *Monowai* is a most comfortable steamer of about 3,500 tons, commanded by one of the most charming captains it has been my good fortune to meet with in my travels. Watching tenderly over his "boarders," always on the outlook for anything which may add to their comfort or contribute to the pleasure of the trip, Captain Carey ought to be surnamed the father of his passengers.

The voyage is far from being uninteresting, for, apart from the pleasure of gliding over a smooth sea, the long and regular swell of which gently rocks one, of watching sunsets of surpassing beauty, or of passing evenings under a firmament literally ablaze with stars, one lands at two veritable earthly paradises—Honolulu, the capital of the Sandwich Islands, and Apia, the chief town of the island of Samoa.

Honolulu is eight days from San Francisco. The

boat stopped seven hours, which gave us time to see the town of Honolulu, and to drive to the Pali, a small mountain, from the summit of which an enchanting view of the whole island is to be had.

Honolulu is a rather Californian town, that reminds one of Los Angeles. A high state of civilization has been reached: you would look in vain among the Sandwichers for a woman wearing a smile and nothing more. The type is a pleasing one: soft, almond-shaped eyes set in an amiable, smiling face meet you at every turn, and there they live, these suave-looking people, far away in the Pacific Ocean, in the midst of sunshine and perfume, in an ideal climate, with a temperature varying from sixty-five to eighty-two degrees from the first of January to the thirty-first of December. Their land is radiant with a thousand flowering shrubs, and stately with palms, cocoanut palms, date palms, and the well-named royal palm that raises its tall, straight trunk like a silver mast high into the air, bearing a drooping crown of graceful leaves at the top.

Graceful, too, are the young women of the people, with their loose, white dress, hanging straight from the neck, unconfined by belt or band, a garment following to a great extent the lines of the Watteau gown. And their charming gait! with what *nonchalant* ease they carry themselves! the supple body balanced with dignity befitting a state procession.

With time at one's disposal, what an agreeable fortnight one could spend at Honolulu, in the most delicious *far niente*, admiring the people, listening to the birds, breathing the perfume of the flowers, swinging in a hammock suspended from two picturesque palms!

But there is the steamer's whistle sounding, and we must go on board. It is with the deepest regret that we leave this little earthly paradise, lit up as it is at our departure by a sunset sky ablaze with gold, emeralds, rubies and topazes. In ten minutes the scene has completely changed. The glory has faded, and all is rapidly being steeped in profound darkness, for, in the region of the tropics, there is scarcely any twilight. And now we have once more left the land behind, and again become a tiny black spot cast on the immensity of the ocean.

Nine days' good steaming, and we ought to reach the Samoan Islands; but in the interval we pass the equator (an important event), and we are to make acquaintance with the Southern Cross, the famous constellation we have heard so much about, and of which the Australians are so proud that they have transferred it to their national coat of arms—a magnificent cross, they say, that illuminates the southern hemisphere. At last, then, we were going to see it for ourselves—this Southern Cross. We counted the days, and every evening, on turning in, we said to each other, " Three days more; two days more," and, at last, " It is to-morrow that we are to behold this marvel." I really believe that we lay awake that night thinking of it. Truth to tell, an Englishman on board, who had been round the world several times, had said to me, " The Southern Cross? Yes, it is not bad." But there are Englishmen whom nothing can move to enthusiasm, and who will exclaim, in front of Vesuvius in eruption, " Yes, it isn't bad," as if they were looking at the belching chimneys of Birmingham. I had been led to expect a grand sight, and a grand sight I expected.

On the 11th of April, 1892 (such dates are epochs in one's life), the captain said to us at breakfast, "This evening at six o'clock the Southern Cross will be visible." The day promised to be a superb one.

Ah, with what impatience we awaited the evening! At last the sun descended to the horizon, and in a few minutes there was a perfectly clear firmament overhead. First, I went aft, to once more look on the Great Bear, and then rejoined the other passengers, who had taken up a post of observation on the bridge. I could see nothing remarkable. I strained my eyes almost out of their sockets. Still nothing.

Up came the captain.

"And this Southern Cross," I exclaimed, "where is it?"

"Why, there it is," replied the captain, stretching out his hand toward the horizon.

"But where?"

"Why, bless me, don't you see it? Look there— where I am pointing. There is one star, that is the foot of the cross; there is another, that forms the head; then there are a third and fourth, forming the arms." And then, pointing them out successively, he repeated, "One, two, three, four."

Now, really, a fakir who had just heard that he would never see Vishnu, could scarcely pull such a long face as we did when we found out how hugely we had been taken in.

Picture to yourself a cross (for a cross we must admit it to be) of the meagerest dimensions, formed by four stars, which are not of equal magnitude, and of which the fourth, the one that forms the right arm, is not even placed symmetrically!

The Southern Cross must have been discovered and named by some patriotic zealot, who believed that he saw in this cross a sign that John Bull, the Christian *par excellence*, was destined to acquire and convert the Austral hemisphere.

Of all the geese that pass for swans in the Colonies, the Southern Cross is the biggest.

I went to bed that night feeling very " sold," and, throughout the eighteen months that I spent in the Colonies, I never could see the Southern Cross without shaking my fist at it. Was ever anyone so taken in?

A few days later Samoa was to make up to us for the disappointment we had just suffered. We were to see real savages, and a bay which is often compared to the Bay of Naples.

On April 17th, at six o'clock in the morning, we entered the Bay of Apia.

We dressed with all speed, and went on deck. The Samoans had anticipated us. The steamer was besieged by the natives, who had come out from the shore in their boats. Everywhere around, their merchandise was spread out—oranges, bananas, fans, sticks, mats, clubs, and all kinds of curiosities of the country.

The Samoans do not at all resemble their neighbors. It is not the Papuan type met with in the Fiji Islands, or in New Guinea; it is the type that we saw in Honolulu (which we shall meet with again in the Maoris of New Zealand), only rather darker. The costume is lighter and more primitive, for it consists of a kind of long folded towel tied about the loins. The Hawaiians, the Samoans and the Maoris belong to the Indo-European race. Many of the Samoans bear more resemblance to sunburnt Italians than to the natives of Australia, or even the different types of negroes that one finds in Africa. The face is intelligent, the eyes are clear and soft, the forehead high, the nose rather large, and the body superb. The skin is of a pinkish copper shade, very picturesque in the brilliant sunshine. The walk of these people is full of grace and majesty; here are hawkers of oranges and bananas, looking like undressed princes; imposing and picturesque figures, with their curly hair roughed up all over the head, the strong-knit body thrown back, and the line of the spine hollowed out. They roam about the deck with the air of exiled kings smoking their cigar on the Boulevard des Italiens! Nature would appear to have made them all gentlemen. The hair of the Samoans, which is dark in childhood, is daubed with some preparation of lime, with the result that when a boy is about eighteen his head is often a comic sight, the bulk of the hair being of a Titian red and the ends of a fine canary color. It is as if a red-wool mop had been trying to get itself up to resemble a gold-colored wig.

A boat landed us on the island in a few minutes, when we were once in it; but at the foot of the ladder was a clamoring crowd of would-be ferrymen, difficult to deal with, and it was a shock to find that those sweet-looking creatures could use words—English, or, rather, Anglo-Saxon ones—that made one's hair stand on end. We were careful not to pay the boatman on debarking, but only to promise him his money when we returned. This is a useful precaution to take, otherwise he exacts a fabulous sum for taking you on board. The canny individual knows that you must get back to the boat at any price, and if you are not on your guard he takes advantage of you. It is easy to see that these people are being rapidly civilized.

We breakfasted at a little hotel looking on the bay, and there we had the pleasure of making the acquaintance of Mr. Robert Louis Stevenson, the famous novelist, some of whose works will rank among the English classics. Mr. Stevenson has very delicate health; the fine climate of Samoa tempted him to settle there, and for several years he has been living in the hills above Apia, with his family. We found him full of activity, happy, singing the praises of Samoa and the Samoans, and in a state of health which allows him to continue the production of those *chefs-d'œuvre* that are eagerly devoured in England. *The Master of Ballantrae* is a book which will live as long as the *Tom Jones* of Fielding.

After breakfast, which consisted not of a slice of cold missionary *à la moutarde*, but of fresh eggs and good beefsteak, we went on the veranda to smoke and talk, with the magnificent *coup-d'œil* of the blue bay spread out in front of us, and then we left to stroll about the town.

It was Easter Sunday, and we wended our way to the cathedral. All along the road we met the natives, who smiled at us and made signs of friendliness. "Welcome," said some as they passed; "My love to you," said others. What gentle, pretty savages! And how nice the women looked in their loose sacques, like those we saw in Honolulu, their hair tidily bound up, and their rounded figures carried erect! Two or three had adopted European dress, but the effect was very ludicrous. Mrs. Stevenson had told us that it was the ambition of the native women, as soon as they could afford it, to dress in European fashion, but I imagine that since they have seen that lady in the richly embroidered silk gown, made in the native fashion, which she was wearing when she spoke to us, they feel much less inclined to spend their substance on corsets. The chil-

NATIVE HOUSE, SAMOA.

dren, the little boys especially, made us exclaim in admiration. The ladies wanted to kiss them all.

We arrived at the cathedral, a very primitive stone structure, just in time to see the procession enter, and it was a curious sight, that little bit of Rome lost in the Pacific! The bishop officiated; there were the acolytes in scarlet and lace-trimmed linen, the candles, the incense—nothing was wanting, and the scene was most impressive. The edifice was crowded with natives in their most gorgeous-colored raiment, and all with faces full of awe and respect. Some knelt, the greater number crouched, but all the faces had a religious gravity imprinted on them.

We went on our way. A few yards further and we came upon an English missionary singing hymns under a shed. Half a dozen Samoans were joining in, with their cracked, nasal-sounding voices. I do not doubt that the good missionary does his best, and that the Society for the Promulgation of the Gospel in Foreign Parts believes that he is making converts by the thousand. The contrast appeared to me as ridiculous as one which so vexes, yet amuses, any artistic visitor to Rouen, where, almost under the shadow of the cathedral, a masterpiece of stone carving, stands a little square shanty in brick, with the inscription, *Wesleyan Church*. How many Englishmen with a little artistic feeling, have told me the pleasure it would give them to kick it over and hide it under the earth!

At noon the heat was intense, and we were glad to get back to the *Monowai* for refreshment and the shade of the awning. At lunch time, the Samoans were ordered to pack up their goods and quit the ship.

When the crowd was dispersing, we threw them money from the deck for the fun of seeing them dive to the bottom of the bay and pick up the coins, not one of which they missed. The Samoans can swim before they can walk, I believe, and the water of the bay is as clear and limpid as the purest spring water.

Then we watched the swarm of boats steer for the shore and a number of the young Samoans swim back to Apia. We said good-bye to this sweet land with its purple hills, the luxuriant tropical verdure which we were to see no more of for a long time, to the graceful, majestic palms, and, above all, to those amiable, happy people who live on bananas and oranges and cocoanuts, and whose eternal smile seems to thank the Creator for having sent them into a beautiful world.

Nine days more at sea. In five we shall have arrived at Auckland, in the north of New Zealand; four days later we shall be in Sydney.

On the Friday in Easter week we were in Auckland, a town of sixty thousand inhabitants, very thriving looking, and with an exquisitely clean appearance. Situated in the curve of a gulf, and built on several hills, this town, whose importance grows by enchantment, is destined to become, one day, one of the largest commercial centres of the world. The editor of the *New Zealand Herald*, a most important New Zealand newspaper, had been kind enough to come to meet us at the quay. We went with him in a carriage to the top of Mount Eden, an extinct volcano, and once there we were able to feast our eyes upon a glorious panorama of green pastures, beautifully kept gardens, coquettish villas, a superb harbor, and the ocean to right and left. Only two or three miles separate East from West Auckland, and to reach the town from the south, by sea, you may follow the coast on the one side or the other; but to go from East Auckland to West Auckland by sea would take several days, whether you went round the northern or the southern part of the island.

But we shall come back to New Zealand and shall revisit Auckland.

At six o'clock in the evening we rejoined the *Monowai*, which was soon to land us at our destination. But alas! our delightful days were finished. From San Francisco to Auckland we had been thirty-two passengers in first class. We had all made acquaintance with one another, and we formed a happy and united band. On returning on board we found the boat invaded by about sixty intruders, who had come to join us and get carried to Sydney. Up to this we had, most of us, had separate cabins; now, each was obliged to share it with a stranger. We cast appealing looks at the captain; we would fain have asked his permission to throw all those people overboard, and we one and all made a resolution not to address a word to the new-comers, but to "boycott" and keep them at a distance—as respectful as the width of the cabins would allow.

And now, no more Pacific Ocean: the sea between Australia and New Zealand is generally very disagreeable. A bad sea and a crowded boat, there remained nothing now but the hope of shortly reaching Sydney to keep us in good humor.

On the Tuesday following, at four in the afternoon, we caught sight of the Australian coast. At five we were steaming in at the narrow and imposing passage between great steep cliffs, which forms the entrance to Sydney harbor.

CHAPTER VI.

Sydney—I Have Seen the Harbor—The Australia Hotel—The French in Sydney—The Town—The Parks—Cupid in the Open Air—Little Clandestine Visits to the South Head—" Engaged "— Melbourne— Activity — All Scottish—The Holy Tartufes—Adelaide—Brisbane—Ballarat—Bendigo—Geelong.

THE two finest harbors in the world are those of Rio de Janeiro and of Sydney: but the light is generally defective in Rio, and the misty atmosphere hinders one from seeing all the details of the landscape at one time. In Sydney, the air is so clear that no detail escapes one; everything is sharply outlined; the harbor, with its two hundred miles of indented coast, is stretched out before the eyes of the spectator in infinite meanderings, presenting a new surprise at each turn. It is a succession of transformation scenes. This harbor is incontestably one of the most imposing-looking of nature's marvels. The narrow entrance between two bold headlands is about half an hour's steaming from the city, which seems reposing on the water in the far end of an immense broken-coasted lake. From the bridge of the *Monowai* we are shown by Captain Carey the *cul de sac* where the unfortunate *Dunbar* was wrecked with her great cargo of human souls. The entrance of this trap bears a great resemblance to Sydney Heads, and the commander of the *Dunbar*, further mystified by a thick, dirty night, mistook the one for the other, and steered the unhappy people to their doom. But now we are steaming cautiously between th great sheer cliffs that form the real entrance to Sydney harbor, and in a few moments there bursts upon our delighted eyes a glorious panorama. We are in raptures and we do not miss a bit of it. It is not only the details that charm, it is the *ensemble*. The eye is carried constantly

NORTH HEAD, SYDNEY.

from each separate part to the whole. Each little bay and cove is lovely, and charms the sight, but the whole, the immense, grandiose whole, absorbs one.

Here it is a rugged hill with trees that seem to have their roots in the water; there it is an inviting-looking beach; further on it is a noble hill, its sides dotted over with dainty dwellings, pretty houses, each set in a garden, where the picturesque sub-tropical vegetation, the magnolia, the tree ferns, the cactus and a hundred other such plants are mingled with the loveliest flowers of Europe.

After four weeks of solitude on the ocean, here we are in the midst of life again. Ferry-boats are crossing one another in all directions, plying between the city and the various suburbs. There are numbers of liners at anchor. We pass the Australian fleet. Finally, after half an hour, which passes like a dream, we are alongside the wharf at the foot of the town. We shake hands with Captain Carey and our fellow-passengers, throw a last glance of contempt at the Auckland intruders, and go on shore.

My impresario and his son and some dear friends had come to meet us. They did not say, "What kind of passage have you had?" or "How are you?" Nothing of the kind; it was, "What do you think of the harbor?" Some journalists, too, have come to welcome us. They crowd around, crying in chorus, "Well, and what do you think of the harbor?" It is evident that this harbor business is going to be terribly overdone. "Your harbor is a beauty, no one denies that," I feel inclined to exclaim; "but, after all, you did not make it."

I hope I am not going to be pursued and overpowered with the Sydney harbor, for I want to be able to keep it as one of my finest souvenirs of travel. It is with certain fine bits of scenery as it is with the tunes of *Il Trovatore;* by dint of hearing too much of them, one ends by cordially hating them. An idea! I will get a card printed and wear it through Sydney streets: "Your harbor is the finest in the world."

The luggage examined, we speed away to the Australia Hotel, which we reach in a few minutes. Another agreeable surprise. The Australia Hotel, where a suite of pretty rooms has been engaged for us, is a revelation. Neither Europe nor America has anything more comfortable and luxurious to show. The rooms are elegantly furnished, the table excellent, the wines first-class, the manager most obliging, the service admirable. We are going to be in clover. The Australia is a happy combination of the best features of European and American hotels. Sydney has as much right to be proud of this hotel as of her harbor: and she made it!

Next morning, by the kind invitation of Lord and Lady Jersey, we lunch at Government House, and in the evening we are dined, or rather banqueted, by the Cosmopolitan Club. Sydney society hastens to welcome us, and invitations to dinners, dances, lunches, picnics, pour in from all sides. The Mayor and his charming wife invite us to go and hear the organ in the Town Hall; in a word, the Australians seem determined to show us that they deserve their reputation for being the most hospitable people in the world.

The banquet at the Cosmopolitan Club was presided over by the Mayor and followed by an improvised concert, at which we heard some high-class musicians, all, or almost all, of them French: M. Henri Kowalski, a pianist, known far beyond the Australian continent; M. Poussard, the violinist; M. Deslouis, the fine baritone; Madame Charbonnet, the distinguished pianist. Music is in good hands in Sydney, for it is in the hands of French artists. The next day I met at the Town Hall Monseigneur Moran, Cardinal Archbishop of Sydney,

Monseigneur Carr, Archbishop of Melbourne, and several other prelates. The building is magnificent, the main hall a superb one. There, again, I was proud to learn that the beautiful window had been designed by a compatriot of mine, M. Lucien Henri, who has adapted the thousand strange and beautiful forms of Australian *flora* and *fauna* to architectural purposes. With M. Henri this has been a labor of love which has absorbed his brain for years, and I was glad to learn that the New South Wales Government had pledged itself to take two hundred copies of the truly great work he has prepared on the subject.

As for the organ, everyone knows it is the most complete that exists. The organist, M. Wiegand, a Belgian, almost a Frenchman, executed several pieces, which showed to advantage the player and the instrument.

Sydney is a town of about four hundred thousand inhabitants, well built, possessing several fine buildings, among which may be named the Post Office, the Town Hall and the Parliament Houses; it has pretty theatres, parks and public gardens. If the town were built like an amphitheatre around the bay it might be classed among the loveliest in the world; but the harbor is only seen in the elegant suburbs of Darling Point, Pott's Point, Elizabeth Bay, Rose Bay, etc. The city proper is built pretty much on the flat in the hollow of the gulf, and bears a striking resemblance to some of the towns of Lancashire and Yorkshire, such as Manchester, Leeds or Bradford. But if the town strikes you as merely one more gigantic monument erected to British activity— just think a moment, a town of four hundred thousand inhabitants, where sixty years ago there were but a few convicts—the suburbs, built upon the points that jut out into the harbor, arrest your admiration by their surprising beauty. Many of the houses here are perfect little palaces, among others, the one which was inhabited when I was in Sydney by Lady Martin, widow of the great Australian jurisconsult. The view from the house and grounds was fairy-like in its beauty, and wherever

VIEW OF SYDNEY FROM LAVENDER BAY.

one turned in the suburbs of Sydney fresh beauties of scene met the eye.

In the Museum, a great shanty in brick which disfigures the park, is to be found a collection of pictures signed by some of the greatest masters; but the thing which struck me as most noteworthy was a collection of water-colors, of which the director, Mr. Montefiore, himself an artist of talent, has a right to be proud.

In spite of the lovely climate which Sydney enjoys, the parks are not frequented by society. You look in vain for cafés or any attraction of that kind. They are simply great fields, rather well kept, where, as in London parks, meet together the street orators, the socialists, the anarchists and the unemployed. This by day. As night comes on, their place is taken by lovers who come to "coo" to one another on the benches or loll about on the grass. But if the parks have no attraction for us, the Botanical Garden more than makes amends. How lovely it is! Situated in a bend of the harbor and gently sloping to the water's edge, planted with the rarest trees and flowers, ornamented with pretty statues, I know nothing of the kind that can compare with it. In spite of all this, one does not see many people about the gardens, and when I went there for my favorite walk, I could carry on my meditations perfectly undisturbed. A couple of lovers on a bench, laced in each other's arms and gazing in each other's eyes without uttering a word, a poor wretch lying on another bench, trying to forget in slumber a night passed in the open air, and a morning perhaps breakfastless, a few loiterers in the walks; but no pretty toilettes, nothing to denote the existence of a rich and elegant town a hundred yards off.

Australia, like England, is the country of out-of-door love-making. Everyone to his taste. A deputation of scandalized people one day presented themselves before one of the cabinet ministers to beg that he would have the park gates closed at sundown.

"I shall do nothing of the kind," he answered. "Leave those poor things alone. If you feel shocked, avoid the parks at night or stay in your own houses."

For that matter this is the tacit reply which the London police makes to the reiterated complaints made by the public on the subject of the things that take place and are tolerated in the parks of the capital of the "moral country" *par excellence.*

The Sydney parks, frequented by the lower classes, are not the only spots consecrated to Venus. The better-class, if not better-motived couples, quit the town and push on to the South Head, which forms one of the majestic pillars of the harbor entrance. It is a sight to see the procession of cabs with drawn blinds gently trotting to Bondi, to Coogee, to South Head, and all those mysterious Cytheras. Arrived at their destination the couples leave the cabs, the lady closely veiled and walking with the modest bearing of a Sunday-school teacher, and wander away in the scrub, the thick, discreet scrub that abounds all around. These couples, to judge by their appearance, belong to the superior classes.

Take a walk with a lady in these parts and no one will take any notice of you. You will be regarded with a look which seems to say, " You know what we are up to ; we know what you have come for ; do not let us interfere with one another." But do not venture there alone, as I once did, drawn by a curiosity to verify the hundred-and-one stories that had been whispered to me, for you will be received like a dog in a skittle alley, and at every turn you will be repulsed with " Engaged ! "

These sentimental promenades generally take place in the morning between ten and one, that is to say, at the time of day when papas and husbands are busy in the city. This shows plainly that the drawn cab-blinds do not screen young, affianced couples, to whom British custom allows so much liberty that thanks to it they can conduct their love affairs in public without having to lower their eyes, much less the blinds of a cab.

Impossible to speak of Sydney cabs without asking why this city does not possess a single cab holding more than two people. It is not everybody who wants to go to South Head, after all! If you happen to be three or four going to a ball or a theatre you must take two cabs ; if you have to go to the station with six trunks, you must take six cabs. Sydney is probably the only important town in the world that has no public carriages with four places.

After a three weeks' sojourn in Sydney, I left with great regret the charming people who had given me such a hearty reception ; I left the Australia feeling pretty certain that I should not again find such accommodation in any hotel in the Colonies. On arriving at the station to take the train for Melbourne, we found the director of the line, the station master and several other important officials waiting to put us into a reserved carriage and to wish us a good journey. Friends had brought bouquets for the ladies, and when the train started we carried away with us a most delightful memory of Sydney.

The journey from Sydney to Melbourne takes eighteen hours and calls for no notice. Flat stretches of country everywhere, studded with the eternal gum-tree and nothing else. At five in the morning you must turn out of your sleeping car to change trains at Albury Station. You are on the frontier of the colony of Victoria, and the gauge is not the same as you have been traveling on. Do not, on account of this, be led to believe that you are about to penetrate into an enemy's country. There never has been any war between New South Wales and Victoria, but simply a mean jealousy which shows itself in all kinds of reprisals. The New South Wales man says to the Victorian, " To come into my country you shall be made to turn out of your berth at five o'clock in the morning." " I don't mind," replies the Victorian; "to come my way you will have to do the same. We are quits!" All the policy of these two countries may be summed up in the two phrases.

The express train arrives at Melbourne at a quarter-past eleven in the morning, in a station which would disgrace an European town of fifteen thousand inhabitants. The reason, do you ask? Simply this, that absurd sums have had to be spent to satisfy the jealous rivalries of the small towns and give them finely built stations, some of them ridiculously important looking, and that there is no money left for the two metropolitan towns, which have plenty of business to look after and so do not torment the Government.

There is no difficulty here in procuring cabs, which are not the hansoms of Sydney, but little *chars-à-bancs* for four persons, roofed with a tarpaulin cover like a grocer's cart, and provided with two steps, very high, very narrow, and placed one above the other, perpendicularly, which makes entrance difficult, and descent dangerous.

The Grand Hotel, situated opposite the Houses of Parliament and public gardens, is comfortable, but after the Australia of Sydney, what a come-down! The cuisine is not bad, but neither wine, beer, nor alcoholic beverage is sold under the roof of the Grand. One has to order it in from a wine merchant's, at the risk of making oneself conspicuous in the eyes of all the water drinkers and tea tipplers.

The city of Melbourne was founded in 1835, and its population has increased with marvelous strides. To-day Melbourne has more than five hundred thousand

TOWN HALL AND SWANSTON STREET, MELBOURNE.
[*From a Photograph by* LINDT, *Melbourne.*]

inhabitants; the population of the entire colony being only eleven hundred thousand. Thus, the capital is as populous as the rest of the colony. In New South Wales, South Australia, Western Australia and Queensland we find the same state of things. It is only in New Zealand and South Africa that we find the population spread over the land.

Melbourne cannot boast of any site that is worth visiting; but, as a Melbournian one day said to me, "Melbourne can afford to do without scenery."

The city, with its activity, its broad, straight streets, its high buildings, its magnificent system of cable trams, is essentially American. In Collins street you can easily fancy yourself in New York or Chicago. If I were not always so faithful to my first loves I could almost prefer Melbourne to Sydney. Between the two it is hard to express a preference.

In Melbourne I met with the same amiability, the same hospitality as at Sydney. I found there a choice and intelligent society, and a people perhaps more active than those of Sydney. For instance, the Alliance Française, which kindly gave us a reception, has nearly five hundred members. The Austral Salon, to whom, also, I owe a charming afternoon, is composed of ladies and gentlemen, lovers of literature and art, who meet together to read and discuss literary masterpieces. Just as in America, one finds here intellectual life without pedantry.

Mention must be made of a few public buildings which are imposing-looking: the Town Hall, the Post Office, the Parliament Houses, the Treasury, the Banks and a Museum already rich in treasures. Government House, which is about half a mile from the town, is larger than that of Sydney, but neither so picturesque nor so well situated. The ballroom is immense— quite as large as that of Buckingham Palace. The honors are done by the most popular of all the Colonial Governors, and his wife, the lovely Countess of Hopetoun. When I have said that Melbourne possesses pretty public gardens and elegant suburbs, I shall have almost exhausted the notes that I took in that city.

Here, as well as in the other Colonies, I cannot help being struck with the fact that the English Colonies are in the hands of the Scots. Out of seven Governors five are Scottish; the President of the Legislative Council is a Scot, and so are three-fourths of the Councilors; the Mayor of Melbourne is of the same nationality, and the Agent-General in London is another Scotsman.* England ought not to call her Colonies *Greater Britain*, but *Greater Scotland*, and the United States might be named *Greater Ireland*. As for the south of New Zealand, it is as Scotch as Edinburgh, and more Scotch than Glasgow. Go to Broken Hill, the richest silver mine in the world, and you will see five great shafts leading to the treasures of the earth; these five great shafts bear the following names: Drew, MacIntyre, MacGregor, Jamieson and MacCullock, five Scots. It is the same thing everywhere.

Melbourne, the intelligent, the much-alive, closes its museums on Sundays. A deputation one day waited upon Sir Graham Berry, then Prime Minister of the colony, to ask him to close the taverns on Sunday. The deputation was chiefly composed of pastors belonging to all kinds of Nonconformist churches. "I am very willing," said Sir Graham, "to use my influence to try and get the taverns closed on Sundays, if you will consent to my using the same influence to get the museums opened instead." The reverend gentlemen appeared not to relish the terms, and as the Prime Minister did not hear any more from them, it must be presumed

*Since replaced by another Scot.

that they preferred the public-house to the museums as a Sunday resort for the people. In England every intelligent person is clamoring for the opening of the museums on Sunday, and they will succeed one day in obtaining what they ask; but it takes time, for the combat has to be carried on against all the allied forces of bigotry and conservatism. And yet it was the first and greatest of Protestants, Martin Luther himself, who said on this very subject, "If anywhere the day is made holy for the mere day's sake, then I command you to work on it, ride on it, dance on it, do anything that will reprove this encroachment on Christian spirit and liberty." The Germans are mostly Protestants, but on Sundays, on leaving church, they go in crowds to visit their museums before returning home. Narrow Sabbatarianism is neither Protestant nor Christian; it is a Jewish institution. But Luther is not for England and Scotland, nor the Colonies. What they prefer is Calvin, John Knox, and all the enemies of simple joys and innocent recreations.

I repeat, the population of Melbourne is more than five hundred thousand souls, but, like Sydney, she could spare a hundred thousand to the Bush without being any the worse for the process. I know no large town in the world containing so many parasites, drunkards, and loafers who have taken root there, but only cumber the ground. They are creatures who prefer idleness with poverty to hard work with a competency, which they could easily find away from the large towns. When I was in Melbourne the Government had opened a bureau to provide work for the unemployed. One day it was announced at the bureau that ten navvies were required

to begin the making of a road about sixty miles from
Melbourne. The workmen presented themselves at the
office, and their names were called according to the date
of their inscription. The secretary had to call over
more than four hundred names before he could get ten
men who would make up their minds to leave the town
to go to work in the country. Sydney and Melbourne
are being crowded to the detriment of the country at
large, which bemoans not having enough hands to develop its resources. One cannot help wondering why, in
a country where the Government makes grants of land at
the rate of five shillings an acre, the desire of every emi-
grant, every town workman, is not to put by a few
pounds, and to become by his own exertions an independent person and a landowner. The Germans do it;
the Italians, the Swedes, and the Scotch do it, but the
English and the Irish seem to prefer to tighten their
belts, and lounge about the corners of the public-houses
in Sydney and Melbourne.

I cannot leave Melbourne without expressing my
thanks to the genial French Consul, M. Léon Déjardin,
who gave me a most cordial welcome, helped me with
his good advice, and gave me valuable information on
the subject of Australia.

The journey from Melbourne to Adelaide is just like
the one from Sydney to Melbourne, a monotonous
eighteen hours' journey through the eucalyptus. However, an hour before you reach Adelaide the country becomes more hilly, the forest grows thicker, and when,
from the last hill, you look down on Adelaide the view
is magnificent.

Adelaide, a town of a hundred thousand inhabitants,

has not yet attained such an importance as Sydney or Melbourne, but it is making giant strides, and, thanks to its cereals, its vineyards, and its mines, it is destined to become the equal of these two great cities. To my taste, it is the prettiest of the three. Adelaide is built in blocks, American fashion, and is surrounded by su-

VICTORIA SQUARE, FROM P. O. TOWER, ADELAIDE
[*From a Photograph by* LINDT, *Melbourne.*]

perb parks. Beyond this it is hedged around with blue mountains, but the town is so clean, so coquettish-looking, so neat, its general appearance so gay, that you forget the landscape, and think of the comfort that must be found in all those attractive-looking houses. Around about all looks prosperous and fertile : golden corn fields, vines, orange-trees bending under their wealth of fruit, rich pastures, mines of gold, silver, and copper almost in the neighborhood; this is what you admire about Adelaide much more than its Post Office or its Town Hall.

I passed a week most agreeably in this pretty city, thanks in part, it must be admitted, to the cordial reception extended to me by the Governor and Lady Kintore, the Lieutenant-Governor (Chief Justice Way) and many others whom it would be impossible to name.

If Melbourne boasts of its tramways, Sydney of its harbor, and Adelaide of its parks, I believe Brisbane, the capital of Queensland, boasts of its river. At Brisbane you are close to the tropics; the eucalyptus is still much to the fore, but the vegetation of the tropics at last breaks the monotony of the scene, and the eye, tired of the gray-green gum-tree, rests with delight upon these luxuriant growths.

Apart from the Botanical Gardens, which are good, the town contains little that is likely to interest an European. The Parliament House is a fine building, and there is a magnificent new Treasury, not yet in use, though long since completed.

Among the towns of secondary importance, towns of from twenty to fifty thousand inhabitants, we have only to mention Newcastle in New South Wales, at one time prosperous and famous for its coal mines, but to-day, thanks to strikes, dull, dreary, and poor, Bendigo, Ballarat, and Geelong, in the colony of Victoria. Bendigo and Ballarat, where more than $150,000,000 of gold were found in thirty years, have retained some traces of their former opulence. They possess superb public gardens, some fine edifices, and beautiful statues. The main street of Ballarat is of an extraordinary width, and is the finest to be seen in the Colonies.

Australian towns have not generally any history. Ballarat is an exception. It was there that the miners, headed by Peter Lalor, sustained a bloody siege against the English troops in 1854. They were beaten, but their rights were acknowledged, and their defeat turned into a victory. Peter Lalor, wounded in the shoulder, took refuge in the Bush. A price was put on his head, but he managed to escape pursuit, and after the general amnesty, he became successively Member of Parliament, Minister and President of the Legislative Assembly of Victoria. Ballarat has just erected to him a statue which has come from the studio of my talented friend, Nelson MacLean.

At the present day Ballarat is as dead as a dowager, that is to say, as a woman *who was*.

In the Town Hall, you will find the walls of the main hall hung with oleographs representing the Queen, the Prince of Wales—such things as tradesmen send their customers at Christmas. It is pathetic.

" How can you put such horrors on the walls of such a beautiful hall?" I asked the Town Clerk who kindly accompanied me.

" What would you have us do?" he said. " We cannot afford to buy paintings. These are better than nothing, aren't they?"

It reminded me of a reply I got from a man in America who was selling jewelry set with sham gems.

" Does anybody really buy those things?" I asked him.

"Of course they do," he replied. "What are the women to do who haven't the money to buy real diamonds?"

However, I must add that the Museum contains many valuable pictures, and I saw more works of art in Ballarat than in any town of the same size.

Bendigo, the other gold-mining town, is more lively than Ballarat, but not so pretty. However, it has a very fine Square, surrounded with buildings which would do honor to a more important town. It has also a labyrinth of ferns which I recommend to lovers in search of a quiet retreat, fresh and inviting. For that matter, heaven knows it is made use enough of, and needs not my recommendation!

Geelong is a sleepy little place, given up to the narrowest bigotry. It, like Melbourne, is situated on the coast of Phillip's Bay.

It is in this city of saints (each colony seems to boast one) that one of the notable inhabitants, an antediluvian fossil, went to the booking office to ask, before taking tickets for my lectures, if it was not dangerous to take ladies to hear "that Frenchman." It was also in this interesting town that an anonymous wag sent me the portrait of Wellington, advising me to place it where I should never lose sight of it. Would it not have been more polite and more Christian to send to a Frenchman passing through Geelong a portrait of General Bosquet, for instance, who, at the battle of Inkermann, saved the lives of a whole division of English who were going to be massacred to the last man by the Russians?

Geelong was intended to be the capital of Australia, and, who knows, perhaps of the world; but—how did it happen? I know not—it is Melbourne that is the capital of the colony, and Geelong, after having held almost in its grasp the pivot of the universe, remains—Geelong.

Sic transit gloria mundi.

CHAPTER VII.

People of Society, People in Society, and "Society" People—The "Sets"—Society Papers—"Miss D. looked thrillingly lovely in electric blue "—The Australian Women are Beautiful—Imitation of the Old World—A Tasmanian Snob—Darling Point, Pott's Point and Sore Point—A Melbourne Journalist on his Townspeople.

FOR centuries past the Old World has tolerated an idle class in consideration of certain services that it renders to the arts, which it protects, to commerce, which it helps, to elegance, which it inculcates, and to good manners, which it perpetuates, but the young worlds ought to keep all their admiration for self-abnegation, for courage, work and the pride of duty accomplished, and ought not to tolerate any society but one which can boast of contributing to the advancement of its country. Yet there are to be found in Australia, a country which owes its existence and its outlook to valiant pioneers with faces wrinkled by toil and suffering, and arms burnt by the sun, people who are already beginning to boast of not working with their hands, parasites who imitate all the idlers of the Old World, and whose only aim in life is to obtain a footing in a certain "set."

These people, people who have inherited fortunes earned by means of hard work and a life of complete abnegation, already run down the Colonies and would think it beneath them to drink a glass of the excellent wine that Australia produces. They shut their ears to

Madame Melba whilst she was among them and of them, but to-day they would willingly pay five pounds for an orchestra stall, I have no doubt, if the *diva* would go and sing in Melbourne or Sydney.

Colonial society has absolutely nothing original about it. It is content to copy all the shams, all the follies, all the impostures of the Old British World. You will find in the southern hemisphere that venality, adoration of the golden calf, hypocrisy and cant are still more noticeable than in England, and I can assure you that a badly cut coat would be the means of closing more doors upon you than would a doubtful reputation.

And the women of that society! They are sublime with their "sets," even away in little Bush towns!

In a little hole of a country town containing about two thousand inhabitants, I met one day a lady, with whom I entered into conversation by saying that I had met a fellow-townswoman of hers in Sydney, and I added, mentioning the name, "You know her, no doubt?"

"Ye-e-es," said she, as if trying to ransack her memory; "I know her—by name, but she and I do not mix in the same society."

"Just so," I said. "Not in the same set, eh?"

"Precisely."

The select colonial was the wife of an ironmonger of the town.

My dear lady, those women, you understand, could not all be ironmongers' wives!

I know of a Melbourne lady who boasted of being obliged to drop the acquaintance of a charming and distinguished woman, because, said she, "I cannot have hansoms standing at my door on my reception days."

Another said to me one day, "Really, the shopkeeper class is getting intolerable; it is pushing itself into society everywhere." The father of this grand person, I found, himself kept a shop in the environs of Melbourne.

And here let me frankly say that I am getting a little tired of hearing about the modesty and seriousness of the Englishwoman, and of hearing the Frenchwoman called frivolous. Have I not seen at bazaars in England and its Colonies—sanctified fairs organized to provide an organ for the church or a peal of bells for the tower—have we not all seen women and girls conducting themselves with unblushing effrontery to fill the coffers of *the cause?* Have I not seen in shop windows their portraits in low-necked dresses, and with their names attached? "Why not their address?" a Frenchman would say, if such things were seen in France.

Our women, thanks be, are more modest and more serious than that. Not only they do not permit the photographer to exhibit their portraits in his window, but if you go to the Salon and see the portraits of our women painted by Bonnat, Carolus Duran, and the rest, you will never see the name of the original in the catalogue. On the Boulevards, it is true, one sees the photographs of our actresses, with the name of each at the foot of the picture, but that is quite another matter: the profession of the stage obliges those who follow it to keep themselves constantly before the public.

Yes, many voyages in many lands have but strengthened my admiration for the Frenchwoman, that clever, thrifty housekeeper, tactful, cheering wife, dutiful and devoted daughter, and wise and watchful mother, deservedly adored of her children.

But let us return to our sets and snobs.

There exist in the great towns of Australia from five to ten papers, called society papers, which live on that ugly Anglo-Saxon failing, snobbery. This is a word for which an equivalent does not exist in the French language, and I think that our most implacable enemies would admit that we have not the fault itself. Heaven knows we have enough others, but if I sometimes feel proud of my nationality it is, among a hundred other reasons, because we have no society papers. It would concern us little to know that Miss Jones took tea with Miss Robinson on Monday, or that Miss Brown went to Mrs. Smith's dance on Tuesday. It does not interest us to know that " Mrs. A. looked superb in pink at Mrs. B.'s ball," and that " Mrs. C. received her guests with much grace at the entrance to the drawing room," nor does it concern us to know that " Miss D. looked thrillingly lovely in electric blue."

Snobbery is not an Australian characteristic, but an Anglo-Saxon one developed to the extreme in the Colonies. It is noticeable in England, Canada, the United States, and everywhere that the English language is spoken. In all these countries the society paper flourishes.

In Australia it is not only Melbourne, Sydney, and Adelaide that indulge in the luxury. There is scarcely a little suburb which has not its own society paper. It is as if we had a Batignolles *Gazette*, chronicling the doings and sayings of that respectable quarter of Paris.

Imagine a French person reading such a sheet, if it did exist!

The most curious part of it is, that all these Anglo-Saxon society papers adopt the tone of *Censores Morum;* and there is not one of them which does not set up as a weekly Juvenal, at the same time flattering its readers by giving accounts of their doings at home, with details that might well make a self-respecting hostess blush.

In society, in the great towns of Australia, I saw plenty of beautiful women; women with lovely faces surmounting most beautifully moulded forms; but I think I met there some of the most frivolous women to be found anywhere. Balls, dinners, soirées, calls, garden parties, appear to fill the life of hundreds of them. Such women are quite without originality. Their conversation is neither interesting, entertaining, nor natural. The consequence is that social life has neither the refined elegance and witty vivacity of Paris, nor the *verve* and intellectual animation of Boston and New York. The men are too apt to talk finance, wool and mutton; the women to talk dress and scandal, discussing the question whether Mrs. So-and-So belongs to this or that "set."

Happily these have not the whole field to themselves, for there are plenty of people in Australia who, while mixing in society, yet find time to read and think and to lend a helping hand to any good work that needs champions and helpers. And when I have said that I met, in the Colonies, numbers of charming people, as amiable and distinguished as could be desired in the best European society, I hope that will be sufficient to prevent this chapter from being read in a wrong spirit.

So, dear madam, who do me the honor to read me in Sydney or Melbourne, please understand that nothing in this chapter is addressed to you. The society of which I speak is not yours, but the other, the one that is written between inverted commas.

While on the topic of snobs, allow me to illustrate with a personal anecdote.

There existed in Hobart, Tasmania, at the time of my visit there, a weekly rag, which, having learnt that I was once a professor at St. Paul's School, London, thought to insult me by calling me "an usher." I must say it did me no manner of harm: it was one of those would-be insults that hurt the person who utters them more than the one whom they are meant for. This was the only disagreeable note that reached my ears amid a chorus of praise, the only mud splash that I received in the Colonies, and it left no stain. M. Alphonse Daudet, in his *Trente Ans de Paris*, boasts of having been an usher, so I might well be proud of it—if I had been one!

Poor silly snob!

Place two Englishmen on a desert island, and in a little while one of them will have found out that his grandfather was better than the grandfather of the other, and he will have inaugurated an aristocracy in the island, if not started a society paper to record his own doings.

The greater part of would-be society people, in Anglo-Saxon countries above all, pass a great deal of their time in discovering their ancestors, and in growing for themselves a genealogical tree, with the trunk taking root in the Middle Ages. The Australians waste little time on this. Like the rest of the human race, they have ancestors, but some of them would prefer to have none. Their origin in New South Wales and Tasmania is a delicate subject, which must not be touched upon.

Voltaire once said that a man cannot be too careful in the choice of his ancestors. Plenty of colonials have overlooked this sound piece of advice. It is well known, of course, that the first colonials were convicts, and so the Australians naturally interest themselves little in any but the two generations that have preceded them. Yet it must be remembered that, up to sixty or seventy years ago, England transported to Australia poor wretches whose crimes would be punished in the present day with a few days' imprisonment, or even a fine of a few shillings. Moreover, we are entering on an age when people are judged by their own merits, and not by those of their ancestors. Nevertheless, the fact remains.

Sydney aristocracy has taken up its residence in the suburbs of the town, on beautiful promontories commanding a view of the loveliest harbor in the world. These elegant suburbs are called Darling Point, Pott's Point, etc. Darling Point is the fashionable place.

Just opposite this lies Cockatoo Island, where convicts sojourned in days gone by. That is Sore Point.

Botany Bay has ceased to exist for a long time past. It is now Elizabeth Bay, Rose Bay, and many other places affected by people whom I found to be, for the most part, of an amiability and hospitality which I shall never forget.

Mr. James Smith, one of the best-known Australian journalists, commenting on Mr. H. C. J. Lingard's *Juvenal in Melbourne*, says: " There are few cities or communities which afford greater scope for the censor and the satirist than our own; its vices, its religious hypocrisies, its political follies, its social shams, its abject worship of money and what money can buy, its low standard of commercial morality, its debased and debasing taste in the matter of literature, art and music, all invite the lash."

I am happy to be able to say that some of the ugliest things on Mr. James Smith's list did not come under my notice at all in Australia. The things that I have tried to point out are ugly enough; but, after all, they are only foibles, failings, weaknesses. In all my wanderings in Australasia I never saw such things as, unhappily, one hears too much of in the United States—judges and juries who are to be bought; councilmen who go into office to apply the ratepayers' money to the lining of their own pockets instead of to the paving of the public streets. I noticed nothing in Australia which could lead one to suppose that it has not the righteousness which " exalteth a nation."

CHAPTER VIII.

Hospitality in the Colonies—Different People at Home and Abroad—Extreme Courtesy of the Australian—Childishness—Visit to the Four Everlasting Buildings of the Colonial Towns—Impressions—Wild Expenditure—Give Us a Prison—" Who is Bismarck?"—" Don't Know "—In the Olden Time.

LIKE the English at home, the inhabitants of the English Colonies are the most amiable and most hospitable in the world. I say, and repeat emphatically, " like the English at home," for it would be a mistake to judge the English by the specimens one meets traveling on the Continent.

And here, perhaps, a question might be asked : How is it that the English, who are so amiable at home, are often so disagreeable when they are on their travels? And we might, in reply, quote the question that M. Labiche asks in *Le Voyage de M. Perrichon:* " How is it that the French, who are so witty at home, are so stupid abroad?"

If one wants to judge of a man, one must study him at home, when he has his natural surroundings, and he is thoroughly himself. Ignorance of the language, uses and customs of a foreign country make him awkward. Abroad he is playing a *rôle* for which Nature never cast him. Setting aside the perfect gentleman—who is a perfect gentleman everywhere—a man out of his own country is more or less like a fish out of water.

He does not breathe freely, he is out of his element, he is not at his ease, much less at his best. He is not himself. I think God, when he created man, must have said to him, " Thou shalt stay at home."

The Englishman at home pleases me, and I do my best to please him ; but let an Englishman in Paris stop me to ask, without even lifting his hat, " *Où est le roue de Révoley ?* " and he displeases and annoys me, so that I promptly answer, " *Connais pas !* "

Upon my word, I believe that their very looks are changed when they travel. I confess that I never met in England with the red-whiskered men and the long-toothed women who figure as English people in French comic papers; but I must, in justice to our caricaturists, say, that in France, in Switzerland, and wherever the tourist is to be found, I have seen these types by the dozen ; and the most curious part of it is, that numbers of my English friends perfectly agree with me on this point. Explain this phenomenon, O ye readers of riddles !

Just like the English at home, I found the Australians—and, to include the people of New Zealand and Tasmania, I should say the Australasians—great in hospitality. I do not remember, for instance, a single town where, on the day of my arrival, I was not put up at the club of the locality. It was who should give me a drive or a mount, a picnic or a shooting-party. The most hearty invitations were tendered from all sides. In the Bush, it is open-house hospitality ; the stranger may enter and eat ; nay, in many cases sleep, if it please him to do so.

If the people of the Colonies have all the little failings of a young society, they have, without exception, all the qualities. In this they resemble the Americans. And what is Australia but a newer America?

But let us not anticipate.

The fact is, however—so much may be stated to start with—the Australian begins to dislike hearing himself called colonial. He is proud of his country; the spirit of nationality is growing in him day by day, and he is proud to call himself and hear himself called Australian.

He is proud, not only of his country, but of his little town that he has seen spring up through the earth, so to speak, and that he has labored to make flourishing. Like the American, he asks you as you leave the railway carriage, almost before you have had time to shake the dust from your garments, what you think of Australia, of his little town that you have only just set eyes on; and, though the place should consist of but one small street, dotted with wooden cottages, he will offer without delay to take you round and show you the sights of the town. The sights of the town! That is too funny for anything.

People to whom I had never spoken would cross the road to come and say, "Look about you well, sir; you are in the garden of Australia here." Each district in Australia seemed to be "the garden of the Colonies." My response also was stereotyped: "You are right to be proud of your district, which is evidently the most beautiful in the Colonies."

I used to be taken to see little buildings composed of three or four rooms, furnished with a table, four or five benches, a blackboard, and a map. They were called

Technical Schools or Schools of Art. In the vestibule there was always a visitors' book where I was requested to put down my impressions. Making bricks without straw was child's play to this. There was nothing to be done but adopt another stereotyped phrase : "Considering the age of this town, I know few places that have a more promising School of Art." Is it not the counterpart of America, where in the veriest little villages there is sold an album of views of the district? that is to say, photographs of Smith's pharmacy, Jones's drapery establishment, and the hotel kept by Brown.

The happiness of the Australians is something enviable. They are so satisfied with themselves and all that is Australian. When they travel they utter cries of admiration at the sight of a hill that they call a mountain, or a trickling stream that they call a river. It is curious to find a restricted and provincial turn of mind in the inhabitants of such a vast, grand country. If you were not to congratulate them upon the things that they have accomplished, you would be wanting not only in generosity, but in politeness, and I thank heaven that I was able to make some return for the amiability of my hosts, by visiting all the post offices, town halls, hospitals, and technical schools of the different towns.

Among my subjects for the platform was one entitled "The Happiest Nation on Earth." It was a chat on France and the French. I have been traveling about the world a great deal during the past ten years, and have long since come to the conclusion that France, whatever may be her defects, her faults, her vices even, is the happiest of the nations of the globe, and certainly the country where people best understand how to live. An Australian came one evening and sat by me in the smoke-room of a club. "What an astonishing power of observation you have!" he said. "You have not been more than two months in the Colonies, and I see by the papers that you are going to give a lecture on Australia." It was evident that to him the happiest nation on earth could only mean Australia.

Nations are like individuals. When they are young they possess all the characteristics of childhood—curiosity, susceptibility, the love of hearing themselves praised, jealousy of the younger brother or sister if the plums are not distributed with strict impartiality.

I know a little New South Wales town of fifteen or sixteen hundred inhabitants, which, being jealous of its neighbor because a prison had been built for it, insisted that the member of Parliament should obtain from the Government as large and as handsome a prison as that of the neighboring town. As usual, the Government acceded to the demand of the member. This is how big buildings spring up in the Colonies. The electors say to their representative, "If you do not obtain a new Town Hall or Post Office for us, we shall not vote for you and you will lose your seat and your three hundred a year." The member says to the cabinet minister, "I must have a Town Hall for the town that I represent. If you do not give it to me, I shall not vote for you, and you will lose your place and a thousand a year." And thus it is that, in the most insignificant little towns of two thousand inhabitants, in the seven Colonies of Australia, you may see a Town Hall that has cost thirty thousand pounds, a Post Office that has cost twenty thousand pounds, a Court House after the same rate, etc.* To cope with this reckless expenditure the country borrows money, and was last summer in a state bordering on bankruptcy.

The Australians have adopted the device, "Advance, Australia!" but it is John Bull who advances—the funds.

To come back to our little jealous town—it obtained its prison. But when it was completed it remained six months without inmates. What did the townspeople do but hold an indignation meeting, and pass a resolution expressing the hope that the magistrates and the police would henceforward strictly do their duty, so that this deplorable state of things might no longer exist!

There is happiness in believing oneself in possession of what is best in the world, and the Australians enjoy that happiness. They are satisfied with their lot, and no longer concern themselves about the affairs of the Old World, which has ceased to interest them. I was talking one day to an Englishman who had been established in the Colonies nearly fifty years. We talked about Europe, and I had occasion to mention Bismarck and a few other well-known names. I verily believe that he had never heard any of them before. Presently I said to him:

" Perhaps you do not take much interest in the things that are going on in Europe?"

* In Maryborough (Victoria), there was a ceiling bought for the Court House at a cost of £6,000. To put it up, workmen were had over from Germany. The town has not yet four thousand inhabitants.

"My dear sir," he replied, "to tell you the truth, I shall soon have been fifty years in this country, and now I can do without Europe altogether."

The true Australian takes more pleasure in hearing the amateurs of his own particular town than in listening to the great singers whom Europe sends him from time to time. Left to himself, he takes his pleasures at his club, at church bazaars, at meetings social and political—in a word, in everything local.

Open any of the newspapers published in the Colonies, and you will see no European news, so to speak, unless it be in Sydney or Melbourne; but these two cities are not Australia. The real Australia consists of hundreds of little centres of population scattered over a continent of about the same size as the whole of Europe. If, however, an Australian cricket team happens to be in England or America, long cablegrams, at eight shillings a word, keep the Australians posted up in their successes or reverses. The local interest dominates everything. The Americans are more advanced. They have passed through their transformation period. Europe interests them; but it must be added that America is but six days' journey from Europe, whereas from Australia to England is nearly a six weeks' voyage. Besides, Australia is much younger than America.

Yes, it is young, that broad, brave Australia, and when I think of what it has accomplished in a few years, it seems to me that it can afford to laugh at its own little foibles, even as I laugh.

I was one day taking a drive in Broken Hill, the richest place in the world in silver mines—Broken Hill, eight years ago a desert, to-day a town with forty thousand inhabitants. We were passing a little tumble-down building.

"What is that old construction?" I asked my companion, an engineer of the district.

"Oh, that?" he replied. "In the old times it was the Court House."

"In the old times!" I instinctively thought of the days of the Crusaders.

"What do you mean—'in the old times?' But I thought Broken Hill was only about six or seven years old?"

"Oh," said he, carelessly, "I mean three or four years ago."

That is the *olden time* of Australia.

CHAPTER IX.

Colonial "Cheek"—Mutual Admiration Society—An Inquisitive Colonial—A Verbatim Conversation—An Amiable Landlord—Modest Politicians—Advice to England by an Australian Minister — Provincialisms — Napier — Opinions on Madame Sarah Bernhardt — Mr. H. M. Stanley and the Municipal Councilor—The Czar had Better Behave Himself—I Introduce Sophocles to the Colonies and Serve Corneille a Bad Turn—An Invitation Accepted with a Vengeance.

YOU find in the English Colonies all the traits of character possessed by the Americans and all peoples that are relatively very young: not only childishness and irreverence, but self-sufficiency and "cheek."

Each English Colony is a little mutual admiration society, jealous of its neighbors and fully persuaded of its own superiority. The strong provincialism of the Australians proceeds from their isolation and complete ignorance of the Old World. Their self-sufficiency springs from the democratic spirit—the spirit of independence inculcated in them from the tenderest age, and which makes every free-born Briton say, "I am as good as my neighbor," which may be interpreted, "I am a good deal better."

T: is an English sentiment that flourishes in colonial air.

Let the greatest scientific men of England meet at the Mansion House to do homage to M. Pasteur, and publicly acknowledge the complete success of his great discoveries, and you will see in the newspapers next day a letter from some pretentious ignoramus, declaring that M. Pasteur is overpraised and that his discoveries are far from satisfying the writer of the letter.

If a French workman found himself in the Sorbonne or the College de France, and heard a lecture by a Caro or a Renan going on, he would respectfully leave the hall and say to himself, "This is a little beyond you, my boy; you have come to the wrong place." An English workman, an Australian still more, would quit the building in contempt, probably shouting, "What interest can there be in such stuff as that? How does the fellow get anyone to listen to it? He is a fool."

A strong characteristic of the lower-class Australian is irreverence. Not irreverence for many things that still claim obeisance in the Old World. If it were but that, I could almost admire him for it; but, unhappily, he utterly fails in respect for most things that are held, and always will be held, in well-deserved respect in any world worth living in; for instance, such things as old age, talent, hard-earned position. He speaks of his parents as "the old man and the old woman;" and if he is not quite sure of being able to write lines as fine as Shakespeare's, it is because he has never tried.

In England, the people of the lowest class often speak of their children as "encumbrance." In Australia it is the parents who are the encumbrance.

For this spirit of irreverence the parents themselves are largely to blame. They do not subject their children to proper discipline; in fact, young Australia cannot be said to know the meaning of the word "discipline."

What a boon compulsory military training would be to the youth of Australia in making them know what salutary restrictions and perfect, unreasoning obedience mean!

It is to be regretted, too, for his sake, that woman does not make her influence felt enough to act as a subduing, restraining, elevating factor in his existence.

In every corner of the globe where two or three Englishmen have congregated, you find that insupportable person, the man who writes letters to the newspapers to make known his opinions *urbi et orbi*. Political, religious, social, commercial, literary and dramatic questions—all these are within his domain; he is omniscient. The type is to be found in London; in the provinces it is rampant. He decides the greatest State questions, gives advice to the sovereigns of Europe, criticises the achievements of Edison and the discoveries of Pasteur; nothing is sacred from the pen of this conceited wiseacre. He has a remedy for all the evils on earth, and modestly signs his letters *Veritas, Justitia, Observer*, more often *Pro Bono Publico*. These people are the *Perrichons* of Anglo-Saxondom.

What cool impudence, what bounce they have, some of those good Australians!

I was stopped one day in Sydney streets by a young man, rather well dressed, who tapped me on the shoulder and said, " Are you Max O'Rell ? "

" Yes; what do you want with me ? "

" Oh, nothing. I wanted to have a look at you, that's all."

If you are proud and stuck up, do not go to Western

America nor to the Colonies, where you would soon be brought to your bearings. On getting to the hotel of a certain Australian town one day, I inquired for the address of a gentleman for whom I had a letter of introduction.

"Where does Mr. B. live?" I asked.

"Do you mean Dick B.?" replied the landlord. Men are known as Tom, Dick or Harry in the Colonies and "out West."

In another Australian hotel the landlord came to me soon after my arrival and, with a pleasant but somewhat protecting smile, said, "There are about a dozen commercial travelers staying in the house; if you like, I will introduce you to them; perhaps, if you make a good impression on them, they will go to hear you in the Town Hall to-night."

This obliging host wanted to do me a good turn. His intentions were excellent. I thanked him, and declined.

The following is a verbatim account of a conversation overheard in Broken Hill on the day after my first lecture there. The miners were all on strike, and two of them were sitting on a fence, having a quiet chat.

"Well, Bill, what did you do last night?"

"Why, I went to 'ear Mac O'Neil."

"Mac O'Neil? Who the —— is he?"

"Oh, don't yer know? One of Smythe's * lit'ry ——," with an accent of great contempt on the *lit'ry*.

Every Australian goose is a swan at the very least. Just opposite my hotel in Wagga-Wagga (how one

---

* Mr. R. S. Smythe is known to every colonial as the manager of literary men's lecturing tours.

must be handicapped when one hails from Wagga-Wagga !) there were three little shops, one a draper's, another an ironmonger's, the third a grocer's. The first was called Imperial Emporium, the second, Hall of Commerce, the third, Great Commercial Entrepot, pronounced by the inhabitants *Interpott*.

I pass over the Louvres and Bon Marchés of Tarakundra, Maratitipu and Ratatata.

In a town of fifteen hundred inhabitants, I saw inscribed over the door of a little shop where in the window reposed a few pounds of cherries and strawberries, *Palais de Fruits*—in French, if you please.

But what is this compared to the little shop in Invercargill, New Zealand, where cheap toys are retailed, and which bears the proud name of *Leviathan Toy Depot ?*

In the politicians of the Colonies the self-sufficiency becomes epic. A democratic politician is self-sufficient enough anywhere; judge for yourself what he must be in the Colonies.

Sir George Dibbs, Premier of New South Wales, and Knight Commander of St. Michael and St. George, went, in the spring of the year 1892, to pass a few months in England, and to profit by his voyage to enlighten the English Government on colonial matters. For months the Australian newspapers were full of telegrams, descriptive of the doings and sayings of the great statesman. He had dined here, danced there; he had passed several days at the castle of Lord A. or hunted with Lord B.; he had been presented to His Royal Highness the Prince of Wales, and had kissed the hand of the Queen. It was Dibbs, served up with a fresh sauce day after day. Great was the surprise of his admirers at home to read one day that the democrat, the almost republican Australian, had knelt before Her Majesty to receive the order of knighthood. "He deserved it," said some. "Going on as he was, he could not escape it," said others. "Well, it is all over now; the English aristocracy have corrupted him!" Some laughed, some made fun of it; others began to be angry. Cablegrams continued to pour in, but soon announced the return of the new-made knight. Was it a courtier or a faithful colonial that would present himself once more among them?

Sir George came home and reappeared at a great reception held in his honor at the Sydney Town Hall, in his old part of friend of the people. It was not a violet and cherry colored ribbon that had changed him. He had done his best to avoid the bauble. The Queen willed it, and he had to bow to her wishes; he had done it "to oblige the lady." The next thing to do was to explain to the young democracy of Australia the purpose of his voyage. The minister got through this very neatly.

I extract from his modest discourse the following passage:

"I am told other people have tried to do the same thing before me and that I was traveling over old ground. I admit that is quite true. Great events and great success are not achieved by the first attempt. It is not the first broadside that wins the battle, but that continual pegging away which we read of in the life of Abraham Lincoln. I had numerous interviews with Mr. Goschen, and found in him a hard nut to crack. One look at his hard, strong lower jaw told me that I had met a foeman worthy of my steel (*applause*). Mr.

Goschen did not like our fiscal policy. I told him that that was no concern of his, but only the concern of the people of New South Wales (*cheers*), and Mr. Goschen succumbed in very little time."

If England, in her maternal solicitude, offered to lend Mr. Goschen to Australia to reduce its finances to something like order (as he has already been lent to Egypt) the people of the Colonies would reply that Australia possesses Goschens by the dozen, and that John Bull may mind his own business, and keep to his own country.

The Minister for National Defence of one of the Australian colonies (formerly a tradesman) was on the Thames one day with several English officers. He fell to criticising the fortifications and to explaining how easy it would be to take London. The naval and military authoritie listened to the ex-shopkeeper and kept their countenance. The *sang-froid* of the Briton is prodigious. For many a week the anecdote was the delight of the London clubs.

On the occasion of a public holiday-making, the mayor of a little town asked me to accompany him to where the townspeople had assembled to pass the day in merry-making. When we reached the place, a deputation came to welcome His Worship (thus do English mayors modestly compete with the divinity).

Mr. Mayor, without alighting from the carriage, got on his feet and addressed a few impressive phrases to the crowd, who listened in respectful silence.

"Yes, my dear fellow-townsmen," said the worthy mayor, "enjoy yourselves, for you deserve to. Such a hard-working community as this can take its holidays with a light heart and easy conscience. I thank you for the kind words you have addressed to me. I feel them very deeply. As long as I have the honor to be your mayor, you may rest assured that I shall always take an interest in the recreations of the people."

Never did a Royal Highness, opening a public recreation ground, go through his part with more solemnity.

The more isolated the town, the more accentuated the provincialism. On the east coast of New Zealand there is a little town of three or four thousand inhabitants, the personal importance of which is Homeric. The town is Napier.

I had just given a lecture in Wellington, the capital of New Zealand. The hall was crowded, and never did I speak to a warmer or more appreciative audience. As the people were leaving the hall, my manager caught the following scrap of conversation:

"What a success!"

Then followed a few flattering remarks.

"Not bad," said the person addressed; "but it would not do for Napier; we are more difficult to please than that."

My manager never dared take me to Napier. When one has satisfied Paris, London, Edinburgh, Glasgow, Birmingham, Manchester, Liverpool, New York, Boston, Philadelphia, Chicago, San Francisco, Sydney, Melbourne, Adelaide, etc., one is sorry not to be able to add Napier to the list.

It was in Napier that, after the eminent baritone Santley had made his appearance there, a newspaper gave it as its opinion that there were at least twenty amateurs in Napier who could sing quite as well as Santley, and *much louder*.

I should have liked very much to give a lecture in French at Napier. I should probably have heard next day that my French was far from irreproachable.

I one day met a good Australian who lived in a little town of a few hundred inhabitants in the colony of Victoria. He was unable to speak or understand a word of French. He had been to Melbourne to see Madame Sarah Bernhardt play *Adrienne Lecouvreur*.

"Well," said I to him, "what do you think of our great *tragédienne?*"

"Not bad," he replied; "but I think she is much overpraised!"

A few years ago Mr. H. M. Stanley made a lecturing tour in Australia, under the auspices of Mr. R. S. Smythe. A few days before taking Mr. Stanley to Newcastle, New South Wales, Mr. Smythe was in that town making preparations for the great explorer's appearance. He meets a town councilor of his acquaintance. After the exchange of the usual civilities, the town councilor says to the famous lecture manager,

"Well, Mr. Smythe, whom have you brought us this time?"

"I mean to bring Mr. Stanley to Newcastle next week. How do you think he will do in this town?"

"I should not like to say," replied the worthy town councilor. "I have given several lectures in Newcastle myself, and I have never been able to get a good house."

A little newspaper of Nelson, a New Zealand town of about two thousand inhabitants, speaking of a lecture given by Mr. Stanley, remarked that Mr. Stanley was well enough as a lecturer, but that "he was not well up in his subject."

It was this same paper which, upon the expulsion of the Jews by order of the Russian government, published an article entitled, "*Our* Warning to the Czar."

The Czar had better behave himself.

I myself had the happiness of not displeasing the mighty organ of Nelson too much, for it declared that my lectures were "excellent," *but*, "unfortunately, not equally balanced." I was let off easy.

But the best souvenir I have of this kind is perhaps this one :

It was in B., a little town of from twelve to fifteen hundred inhabitants in Cape Colony.

I was to give a public lecture in the Lyric Hall one evening.

Lyric Hall—what a name for it! Four wooden walls outside, benches inside, and at one end a stage framed in with boards, on which a few nymphs and sylphs had been painted after a fashion.

On the right and left were two long panels, bearing the inscriptions, *Music*, *Drama*. Under these headings came some names, five on either side : Shakespeare, Dante, Milton, Molière, and Corneille on the right-hand panel; Beethoven, Berlioz, Wagner, Rossini, and Verdi on the left-hand one.

I went with my manager in the afternoon to see the hall. The proprietor happened to be there. When he had a spare moment, it appeared, he came there to sit and contemplate his handiwork. For it was of his creation, this Lyric Hall; it was he who had built it; he who had suggested the decorations and the inscriptions. The whole thing had sprung from his own brain, and he was not a little proud of it.

I went up to him.

"Allow me," I said, "to thank you for what you have done for France. You wished to choose five of the greatest dramatic poets of the world, and you have given a place to two French ones."

"How do you make that out?" he responded. "Shakespeare is English, Dante Italian, Milton English, *Moliar* French, and *Cornhill* Spanish. That makes only one Frenchman."

I kept my countenance. Did not the Cid make conquests after his death? He had perhaps acquired Corneille for Spain in this little African town.

"I think you are wrong," I ventured timidly, "if I may be so bold as to advance an opinion after yours."

"Oh," said he, "*you* may be mistaken, like other people."

"Certainly; but that which gives a little weight to my opinion is that I was born a few miles from Corneille's native town."

The proprietor of the Lyric Hall said no more, and went away. That evening, after the lecture, he came to me.

"You are right," he said; "*Cornhill* was not Spanish, he was French. I went to the public library, and I found that *Cornhill* was born at *Rouin*."

"At Rouen; if you will excuse my pronunciation."

"Well," he said, "that is very annoying, for now I must take out his name from my list."

"Oh, do not do that!" I cried.

"I must," he replied, with a sad shake of the head.

"Why?"

"Why? Why, I wish to be impartial and fair to all the nations."

"You are right, and I have no more to say."

It was difficult to keep serious; but I am proud of the look of submission with which I accepted the suppression of Corneille.

"And now," said the owner of the Lyric Hall, "I must find another name to replace *Cornhill's*. Have you any to suggest? A German, for instance. Has Germany produced any poet fit to figure on my list?"

I was on the point of suggesting that Germany would be worthily represented by Goethe. "Nonsense!" I said to myself. "Why should I render this service to Germany? No Goethe, no Schiller, no German."

"If I were you," I said, "I would put a Greek. What would you say to Sophocles?"

"Is he good?"

"He was. He wrote a few good things."

"Is he dead?"

"Yes, he died about two thousand three hundred years ago."

"Then he's one of the ancients?"

"Quite antique."

"You guarantee he is good?"

"Yes, as long as the world lasts."

The questioner thanked me, shook hands, and went away.

If ever you go to the little town of B. you will see on the left-hand side of the scene, in the Lyric Hall, under the inscription *Drama*, the five following names: Sophocles, Shakespeare, Dante, Milton, and Molière.

It was I, too, who caused the grave accent to be put over the name of the great French poet. If I did not succeed in keeping the name of Corneille, at any rate I was able to get that of Molière spelled correctly.

For a finish, allow me to give you an amusing sample of colonial *sans gêne*.

It was in the coquettish town of Durban (Natal), in the month of June, 1893. I was to give a lecture on "Her Royal Highness, Woman," one evening, in the Theatre Royal. My manager, profiting by the subject to do a politeness to the pupils of a large college for girls, presented himself in the afternoon at the college, and, asking to see the principal, offered to put several dress-circle seats at her disposal at half price. As he was leaving, he further said, "If you desire that the young ladies should be accompanied, I shall be happy to admit the governesses as friends," which, in theatrical parlance, means *gratis*.

The principal thanked my manager, and accepted his polite offer.

On the evening of the lecture, there arrived from the college *four* pupils and *eleven* governesses.

A few days later, having heard that I had related the anecdote in public, the lady principal was good enough to write and explain the matter. The letter showed good taste. My manager, it appeared, had made the offer too late; she had not had time to mention the thing to her pupils, otherwise she could have sent many more.

Very good; but she had had time to mention it to the governesses.

After all, dear madam, let us have no excuses, I beg; first, because I strongly suspect my manager to have been actuated by a feeling of business, and not of philanthropy. Philanthropy is scarcely in the manager's line.

Besides, dear madam, that is how the British Empire was made, as we all know.

One may say of John Bull, Junior, as of John Bull, Senior:

> "*Laissez lui prendre un pied chez vous,*
> *Il en aura bientôt pris quatre!*"

—and even eleven.

CHAPTER X.

The Curse of the Colonies—A Perfect Gentleman—A Town Full of Animation—A Drunkard Begs Me to Give the Audience a Lecture on Waterloo—A Jolly Fellow—Pater Familias on the Spree—An Ingenious Drunkard—Great Feats—Taverns and Teetotalers—Why there are No Cafés in the Colonies—A Philosopher—Why a Young English Girl Could not get Engaged.

IN Australia drink is the panacea against the dullness of existence, and drunkenness in most classes of colonial society is an evil that is gnawing at the vitals of the country—a national vice. Not the drunkenness that begets gaiety, but a dull and deadly habit which has become second nature, and is therefore incurable and repulsive.*

I was lunching one day in the club of a large city, the members of which belong to the best society of the place. A gentleman, still young and of a decidedly distinguished appearance, was sitting at a neighboring table. When I had finished eating he rose and came and sat near me.

"I have no need of an introduction," he said, "since we are both members of the same club. Let me tell you how pleased I am to make your acquaintance and to shake hands with you. I have been reading the accounts

---

* I see by a book of statistics that the sum spent every ten years in drink is equal to the sum represented by all the gold, iron and coal produced by the country in fifty years.

of your lectures in the papers, and I regret very much not being able to go to hear them."

"Your occupation, no doubt, takes up all your evenings?" I suggested.

"Yes, alas," said he, half sad, half smiling. "To tell you the truth, I am drunk every evening from seven o'clock."

Drunkenness of that description is so repulsive to me that I forthwith left the dining-room.

In the smoke-room I recognized a friend and went to join him.

"Who is that individual?" I asked, indicating my interlocutor, who had just come in.

"Oh," said he, "a charming fellow, very good company, one of the foremost merchants of the town."

"I am sorry to hear it," I replied, and the conversation went no further.

I remember, one night in Sydney, being interrupted in the middle of my lecture on the English. At the close of the proceedings a man in evening dress presented himself in the little green-room behind the platform.

"I have come to apologize," he said. "It was I who interrupted you. I had misunderstood what you said, and I thought I ought to protest."

"No need to offer excuses, my dear sir," I replied. "First of all, I did not in the least know who had interrupted me, and, moreover, I never take any notice of interruptions, which, I must say, are extremely rare."

"You are quite right. Besides," he added, tapping me on the shoulder, "do not bear me ill-will, for, as you see, I am as tipsy as Bacchus."

Indeed he was, and very proud he appeared to be of it. He was a captain in the army.

In the town of X. (Victoria) I had occasion to go and see the mayor. I found him tipsy. On leaving his presence I went to the office of the town clerk. He was tipsy. From there my manager and I went to call upon the director of the principal bank. He was tipsy. The proprietor of the hotel where I was staying was in bed, suffering from *delirium tremens*. The same night, at my lecture, the police had to eject from the front seats two individuals who, by their conduct, were preventing the audience from following me. One was a prominent person in the town, and the other was the worthy representative of the district in Parliament.

In the afternoon, about five o'clock, I went to the club of the town.

"What are you going to have?" asked some of the members of the club who happened to be there.

"Can I have some tea?"

"Some WHAT?" cried they, staring in amazement at me, as if to ask what kind of stuff I was made of.

"Some tea," I repeated, smiling.

"My dear sir, I don't think we keep the article on the premises."

"And if we have it," said another, laughing heartily, "I don't believe there is anyone here who knows how to make it."

Several other members dropped in. The thing was told as a great joke, and I was surrounded and viewed as a curious animal. Stupefaction was stamped on all the faces.

That evening, after my lecture, I returned to the

club and regained the esteem of my amiable hosts by ordering something stronger than tea. I must say, however, that very few of them were in a state to discern clearly what the glass contained.

Now see the pendant of this picture, and make your own comments.

The following incident happened in the same interesting little town of X.

A few days before my arrival my manager's secretary had come to X. to see the posters put up and make the necessary preparations for our arrival. He went to the bill-poster and gave him the order.

"Before accepting the work," said the man, "I must know whether this Frenchman's lectures are moral, and whether there is to be any music. Music, sir, is, like the theatre, one of Satan's snares."

Our agent assured him that there would be no music, and that he could stick the bills in all security.

On the day of the lecture my manager, whom the incident had greatly amused, offered the man a ticket to go and hear me.

"I should like very much to go," said he, "but I could not set foot inside the hall before knowing whether my master could go with me."

"Oh, that is all right," said my manager. "I will give you another ticket for your master. What is he called?"

"His name is Jesus Christ, sir," replied the bill-poster, drawing himself up.

You may imagine the look of his interlocutor.

This is the Anglo-Saxon potion that one is obliged to swallow in every corner of the globe, and these are the people who reproach the French with their gaiety, I had almost said their happiness, and who in the way of distractions have, as Sydney Smith says, discovered only two things, vice and religion.

Occasionally the colonial drunkard strikes a very comic note.

I shall never forget the one in Bendigo, who, installed in one of the foremost seats, shouted at me from his place:

"Leave John Bull alone, you beggar, and give us a lecture on Waterloo!"

As the subject announced for that night's talk was not Waterloo, and one must never change one's subject without giving due notice to the public, it was out of my power to oblige this comical drunkard. But, as he insisted, and the persuasion of his neighbors had not a quieting effect upon him, it became necessary to get a policeman. He allowed himself to be led off without resistance. However, when about half way to the door, he wheeled round toward the audience, and shouted:

"I tell you the man's a fool. He calls himself a Frenchman, and he can't give us a lecture on Waterloo. He'll make no money in Australia, take my word for it."

So saying, he was led out amid the frantic applause of the audience, who had seized the humor of the situation.

And here a striking contrast may be noted. When a Frenchman is drunk, he is generally socialistic, anarchical, revolutionary, and he raves at the top of his voice, "Down with all tyrants!" When the Englishman is in his cups he grows conservative and jingoistic. He will call up the nations to single combat, and if Mr. Gladstone were to fall into his hands he would make short work of him. "Wa'arloo" seems to be still the watchword of quarrelsome Anglo-Saxon drunkards.

Drunkenness does not make the Australian ashamed, no matter to what grade of society he belongs.

I have seen men, scarcely able to stand upon their legs, enter a theatre or a concert-room with their wives and daughters. Some were noisy, and annoyed their neighbors; others went to sleep and were comparatively inoffensive.

In a very well-appointed house I heard a man at table, in the presence of his wife and children, laughingly relate how he had been led home from his club the preceding night by two friends, and put to bed with the greatest difficulty. His wife tried to smile at the description, and the young girls pretended not to be listening.

In a town in New South Wales, a notability of the district tried to insist on preceding me on the platform, in order to make a speech and present me to the audience. He was perfectly drunk, and I had the greatest trouble to get him to go away.

In France, a man who finds himself overcome by drink hides himself. In the Colonies he parades his state, and does not mind showing himself in public with his family. If he proves too noisy, his wife takes him home, to save the policeman the trouble. And when his club-mates see him depart, they merely say to themselves :

" Poor old Dick! he has had a drop too much! Good fellow, Dick! fond of his glass—a jolly good fellow, capital fellow!"

Not only does the drunkard think himself fit to go to entertainments, but he thinks himself fit to entertain.

I was once invited to supper by a rich squatter, whom a policeman had been obliged to remove from the theatre in the middle of my lecture. On getting to the hotel, this "jolly fellow" had taken a short nap, and, feeling a little sobered, sent word, when he heard that I had returned from the theatre, to say that he and his wife would be delighted if I would sup with them in their apartment. We were in the same hotel. The incident was droll, and the situation rather piquant; I accepted. He confided to me that he had driven fifty miles to come to the lecture, and he overpowered me with compliments, punctuated with tipsy hiccoughs. I believe he even had the audacity to tell me how much the lecture had interested and amused him.

He appeared to have clean forgotten the little scene in which he had played a leading rôle at the theatre. But his wife could certainly not have forgotten it, yet she was there at supper, unconcerned, letting him maunder and drivel, and dishonor himself. We drank champagne at supper, and in less than an hour my host was sleeping heavily in an armchair. Not an attempt at excuses on the part of his wife, who seemed to look upon the situation as quite natural, and, for that matter, had probably seen many similar ones.

Next morning, Sunday, at eleven o'clock, I saw the squatter and his wife on their way to church, doubtless to pray and sing hymns in Protestant fashion.

At five, that afternoon, my late host was dead drunk.

I have seen in the hotels of small towns, young men,

sons of well-to-do squatters, come in from the stations around to shake off the dullness of the Bush and amuse themselves in the town. But what amusements could they expect to find? Intellectual or artistic ones, none. They fell back on whiskey, and went in for a bout of drinking, installed themselves at the hotel, and for days together were hardly an hour sober.

It is not uncommon in Australia to see a young man arrive in a town, hand over a cheque for fifty or sixty pounds to the keeper of some hotel, saying to him:

"Let me have as much drink as I want. When I have drunk my cheque, let me know, and I will go home."

At Grafton, a few leagues from the tropics, I saw an old farmer, eighty-four years of age, who had come into the town to pass a few days at the hotel and be drunk from morning to night. His wife had come with him to put him to bed when necessary, and apply something cool to his head.

Drunkenness in cold climates is comprehensible, while reprehensible; it has a pretext; but in hot climates, in the tropics almost, *ennui*—the absence of social, artistic, or intellectual distractions—that is the only possible explanation.

I have seen still better than all this. I saw with my own eyes the following scene:

An individual of about forty, well dressed, with drawn face, haggard eyes, and the sad and sinister expression of a Chinaman in an opium den, presented himself at nine in the morning at the private bar of the hotel which I had put up at in a town on the banks of the Clarence River. He lays down sixpence, and is served with a glass of whiskey. He adds a little water, with a shaking hand carries it to his lips, and at one draft swallows the contents. Then silent, and without lifting his dull, staring eyes from the ground, he goes away. At the expiration of half an hour, he returns and the operation is repeated. Half an hour later he returns again. The hand trembles more and more and seems to refuse to lend itself any longer to the task. The hotel-keeper, who had seen me watch the scene, said:

"In the intervals he goes to another hotel and gets drink. If you have nothing particular to do, remain where you are and you will see something that will repay you for your trouble."

At about half-past twelve, the poor wretch appeared at the bar for the seventh time. The sixpence is planked down; the glass is filled. The hand goes to the glass, but has no longer power to take it. After many efforts, however, the glass is grasped, but the drink cannot be conveyed to the mouth. The drunkard darts a furtive glance to right and left. No one is looking. He draws a long silk handkerchief from his pocket, and passes it around his neck. With his two hands he holds the two extremities. In his right hand he grasps the glass, and, drawing the end which is in his left hand, the ingenious drunkard makes a pulley of the handkerchief, and thus succeeds in conveying the whiskey to his lips. He puts down the glass, drags himself to the door, and edging along by the walls, he finds his way home to get a few hours' repose.

"This thing has been going on for three years," said the landlord, "but the pulley trick he only took up a month ago; it is the last stage. Soon he will no longer be able to swallow, and *delirium tremens* will carry him off."

"Well," I replied, "*bon voyage!* Good riddance!"

I think that is the most repulsive sight that I have seen in all my travels; the look in that man's face will never be effaced from my memory.

Perhaps you will ask at what age the young man of the Colonies begins to get drunk.

On board the boat which brought me from Africa to Europe we had a young man of nineteen, who was helplessly drunk every night from seven o'clock.

After fourteen days' steaming we arrived at Madeira, where we all went ashore. Do you think the young sot made use of the seven or eight hours that the steamer stopped, to explore every corner of the curious, picturesque old town? Do you think he took a drive to the convent, from whence a really charming view is to be had? No, he went direct to a low tavern, and had to be led, or rather carried back to the ship like a pig, if I may use such an expression without too greatly insulting the porcine race.

After the scenes described above, I beg the reader to spare me the task of recounting the drunken scenes I might give him, taken from the lower classes.

In many a community in the far West, labor is made compulsory, and the drunkard who does not correct himself after being warned, is ignominiously driven from the town by his neighbors.

The small centres of population in America do not offer more distractions than the townships of Australia, and yet I have paid three long visits to the United

States without seeing any drunkenness unless it be in the large cities.

Australia is suffering from two scourges—drink and teetotalism. The first brutalizes, the second effeminates. It is curious that the Anglo-Saxon only goes in for extremes, and has no moderation.

Because wine intoxicates, total abstinence societies suppress wine. Why not man?

But, as the good Chinese proverb has it, it is not wine that makes drunk, but vice. Suppress vice, but not wine.

Unhappily, the excellent colonial wines made in Australia and South Africa are not within the reach of the bulk of the people. Picture to yourself a wine-growing country where it is impossible to procure a bottle of wine that is grown on the spot for less than three or four shillings—nay, in many places seven or eight. The consequence is, that with the exception of the large hotels in the big cities, you never see a dining-room where wine is drunk. The bulk of the people drink tea, which destroys their stomach, and whiskey, which destroys the rest. Weak wine and water, that healthful and refreshing drink of the French lower and middle classes, is unknown. It seems as if Anglo-Saxon throats demanded something that burns or rasps.

I said one day to a Melbourne friend: "How is it that here, in this genial climate, where the people should spend half their leisure time out of doors, you have gone in for public-houses, those ignoble English dens in which people must take their drink standing, and in a disgusting atmosphere reeking of alcohol and tobacco smoke? Why, in the parks and great thoroughfares of the town, did you not have pretty cafés as we have on the Continent in Europe, places where you can quietly quench your thirst, and where you may allow yourself the luxury of taking your wife or daughter?"

Why not? Of course I know why not. Because, in the open-air cafés people are seen, whereas in public-houses people are hidden from view. The reason that he gave me is much less flattering for the Anglo-Saxon race than mine is.

"My dear sir," he said to me, "if you only consider the drunkenness that already exists (and which, unhappily, you do not at all exaggerate), although men are obliged to take their drink standing, just imagine what it would be if they could take it sitting at their ease."

Yet this is that same Anglo-Saxon race which perfectly deafens us with the sound of its own praises, and declares that its greatest virtue is self-control. Curious race, that can do nothing moderately, and which sees no other means for suppressing drunkenness than that of keeping the people without decent drinking places, and trying to force them to drink only water!

Two little reminiscences to finish with.

Every one knows that in the Colonies, as in America, there have been great rushes to certain localities in the hope of finding gold, silver, or some other ore. A mere rumor has often caused rushes of this kind. In hot haste tents, huts and houses were put up. The feverish crowd sought for ore; they found it for awhile; then the vein disappeared, and so, gradually, did they also, leaving behind a few poor wretches who had no means of getting away.

The coach I was one day traveling in drew up by the way at a hotel in one of these forsaken towns to allow the passengers to take food. Around and about that hotel the most complete desolation reigned.

"How do you manage to make a living here?" I asked the proprietor of the house. "The place seems to be no longer inhabited."

"Well, I have the passengers of the coach three times a week, and the handful of people who were not able to get away when the stampede took place, come to me."

"But what do they do in this God-forsaken desert?"

"Oh, they drink, and that keeps me going."

They drink, and that keeps me going! What pathos, what tragedy in those few words!

We had, on board a boat by which I traveled, a rich Englishman who passes most of his life at sea. Did he travel for his own pleasure or for the tranquillity of his family? Traveling on the ocean is one way of passing the time, and English people often have funny ideas of enjoyment. They take their pleasures sadly. I really think, however, that this man's presence on board must have seriously contributed to the comfort of several people on land.

From nine o'clock each morning he was drunk, and never, during the whole voyage of nineteen days, did I for one moment see him in a state to converse, much less discuss anything with anyone on board.

This drunkard was accompanied by his daughter, a giddy girl, who yet appeared to be fond of her father, and lavished pretty attentions on him. The rest of her time was filled up with flirtations with one of the young men on board. At the end of ten days the flirtation took a serious turn, and the young couple announced themselves engaged.

It was the ninth time the young girl had made the trip with her father, and I think it was also the ninth time that she had been engaged. In England this kind of thing is tolerated; nay, better than that, there are Englishmen who only love a woman when they know that she has been loved by others. I know one who is very proud to say, " My wife was engaged, first and last, to half the young men of the town, but it was I who carried the day after all, and married her."

On board ship one quickly makes acquaintance; familiarity begins to reign when you have been a day on the ocean, gossiping starts, and everyone knows all about everyone else.

One fine morning the young girl in question came to sit near me on deck and said, laughing heartily as if she were only telling a good joke:

" I have got engaged to Mr. N."

" I congratulate you with all my heart," I rejoined, with anything but a serious look.

" There is only one obstacle to surmount," said she, " and that is the getting my father's consent."

" Oh," I exclaimed, " you are afraid he will refuse ? "

" Oh, not at all; it is not that, but for the consent to have any value, I must try and obtain it when he — "

" When papa is responsible for his words," I put in quickly, so as to spare the poor girl the annoyance of having to finish the sentence.

" That is just the difficulty," she said, sighing.

The poor young girl arrived at port without having been able to surmount the difficulty. Her father was drunk when he embarked, and, constant in his affections, he was drunk when he landed.

CHAPTER XI.

Types—Caprices of Nature—Men and Women—Precocious Children—Prehistoric Dress—Timidity of the Women—I Shock Some Tasmanian Ladies—Anglo-Saxon Contrasts.

LET us take a glance at the strange types and freaks of nature that one meets with in the Colonies, and see what a topsy-turvy world it is.

The kangaroo springs by means of its two hind legs, and supports itself on its tail, which serves as a helm. There are Australian animals that fly without having any wings, and the Australian swan is black. Trees change their bark every year, while their leaves change not. You find in this curious country pears with their eatable part encased in a hard wooden rind, cherries with the stone outside, and trees with their flowers and seeds growing in the leaves. Other trees there are, the politician being the chief, which flower superbly and give great promise of fair fruit, but when fruiting time comes yield mostly husks.

In South Africa, too, there are strange phenomena to be seen. Water is found on the summits of the hills instead of in the valleys. It is in the valleys that you feel the cold; on the mountains you feel the heat. If you are cold at night open the window; if you are too hot by day, close it. Last, but not least, all the nursemaids are boys.

There are giants in *these* days—if you go to Australia for them. At a banquet given by the Mayor of Sydney, I found myself seated between Sir George Dibbs, Premier of New South Wales, and Sir Joseph Abbot, the Speaker of the Legislative Assembly. When these men rose to reply to the toast of their health, the first uplifted six feet three inches of manhood and the second six feet four. Both are products of the soil, superb-looking men, giants in build. I met with a number of others like them.

The children are early developed. I saw in all the colonies, young girls of twelve and thirteen developed like women of twenty, and showing sturdy calves as they marched with straight and independent tread.

In Melbourne, Sidney, Adelaide and all the places close to the sea, I saw beautiful women, clear-complexioned and admirably formed, looking fresh and vigorous. But when you go north and penetrate into the interior, you find many of the faces looking yellow and dry as parchment. And how could it be expected that the freshness and color of youth would remain on the face of a women when the heat and the drought are such that the paint will not remain on the face of a house? Under this burning sun, in this atmosphere that is a stranger to humidity, the white skin turns brown in no time. The neck and forehead get wrinkled. Add to this eyes that express the weariness and dreariness of life in the interior, a mouth that rarely laughs and that has a droop at the corners. The English are not at any time a gay-looking people, and it is not the monotonous existence of the Bush that would be likely to enliven them very much.

The men are not picturesque in this unpicturesque

country. In the south of France, in Italy, in Spain, in Algeria, you may at every turn meet with a head worthy to pose in an artist's studio, though belonging to a man selling wares across the counter of a little shop, and many more that would grace the operatic stage. In England and the Colonies you miss all that; the types are manufactured by the gross. The Bushman wears close-cut hair, moustaches, and short whiskers, lets his arms hang, or carries his hands in his pockets, while he swings nonchalantly and slowly along the road, a wearied look on his face, his tall frame generally thin and often slightly bent. It takes him ten minutes to fill his pipe. He begins by drawing from his pocket a cake of tobacco. Next he takes his knife and slowly cuts the tobacco into thin shavings. This done, he puts knife and cake of tobacco back into his pocket, and rolls the tobacco between his hands for at least five minutes. Time is no object to him. When the tobacco is almost reduced to powder, he takes his pipe, fills it and puts it in his mouth. Then he sets to work to find a match in his pockets. It is generally in the last. By the time the pipe is lit, the operation has lasted ten minutes.

In little out-of-the-way towns, as yet unconnected with the great cities of the Colonies by railway communication, strange types are to be met with : women of fifty with their hair in curls, such as the daughters of Albion affected about sixty years ago, with large-brimmed mushroom hats, crinolines and polonaises, walking with modestly lowered eyes, speaking with subdued voice, and almost ashamed of having spoken at all.

A traveler one day in my hearing asked a lady of about fifty years of age, who, like myself, was staying in the hotel of a little town in the Bush, if she intended to go and hear me in the Town Hall that evening.

"I should very much like to," she replied, "but I do not know any gentleman who could take me."

She dared not venture alone.

I was one day talking with several Tasmanian ladies in the drawing-room of an hotel in Launceston. Tasmania is perhaps the most *rococo* of all the Colonies, but, thanks to the temperate climate, its women are remarkable for their beauty and freshness. Life in France formed the subject of the conversation, and speaking of my own native town I had occasion to say that, among my friends, there was an old lady, now deceased, whose granddaughter was a grandmother. On the last New Year's Day she spent on earth, there were five generations of the family at her table. "And," I added, "if my old friend had only been able to retard her death by three months, she would have seen the sixth."

Thereupon all the eyes were lowered, a good many blushes arose, and I verily believe that two or three ladies tried to hide under the table. I had evidently created a panic. Great heavens! what could I have said to cause it? Later in the evening, the eldest of the party summoned courage enough to come and confess to me that she thought I had been a little too free in my speech.

"Oh! how?" I exclaimed. "I am eager to know."

"You are forgiven: of course we know you are French and you had no intention of shocking us."

"But what did I say? To save my life, I cannot recollect anything that could give the slightest offence."

"Well," said she, lowering her voice, "you made us

all understand that at the time your old friend died, the young woman belonging to the fifth generation was *enceinte*."

Shocking!

Is it possible that this is a people who have chosen for their device *Honi soit qui mal y pense*?

The device of the Anglo-Saxon race ought to be *Quoi que tu entendras, toujours mal y penseras*.

A race made up of the most extraordinary contrasts: a people that can pray and swear in one breath; that devotes its Sabbaths to the spiritual and the spirituous—the church service and the hideous orgie of the tavern.

In most of the colonial museums the statues which serve as models for the students are nude; but when the hour for opening the museum to the public arrives, the superintendent takes from a cupboard a few fig leaves of ample dimensions, by means of which he veils the too startling nudities. As if a statue could be an object of scandal! On the other hand, men perfectly naked are to be seen bathing in the rivers, and neither the police nor the public seem to be shocked at it. In stations and hotels you will see the walls of certain places covered with inscriptions in pencil, such as, "God loves you," "God waits for you," beside nameless indecencies accompanied by illustrations that would sicken the soul of our lowest rough.

In your hotel you find on the wall an illuminated card bearing the words, "I will lay me down in peace and take my rest, for it is thou, Lord, only that makest me to dwell in safety." Near it, another card bearing the most practical advice, "The proprietor does not hold himself responsible for the loss of valuables left in the bedrooms, and requests visitors to lock and bolt their doors at night."

In the bedroom of a rich and distinguished Englishman I saw over the mantelpiece three pictures: the first was a pretty reproduction of Holman Hunt's beautiful picture, "The Light of the World," Christ knocking at the sinner's door, with a lantern in his hand; on either side of this picture of Christ hung a music-hall beauty in tights, and very *décolletée*. It was not Christ between two *larrons*, but between two *luronnes*.

An Australian, with whom I was one day talking on matters theological, wanted to quote a text from the Bible, which should enlighten the subject for me. He ransacked his memory in vain; he could not remember the verse. "How is it that I cannot recollect that —— text?" exclaimed my theologian.

In another line one finds much the same contrasts in Italy. A workman who enters a wine-shop addresses the keeper of it as *Signor Padrone*, and his waiter as *Signor Primo*; but if one or the other of them should take it upon them to contradict him on any point, this same workman begins such a volley of abuse as would make the bravest navvy quake in his shoes.

CHAPTER XII.

The Bush—The Eucalyptus—The Climate—Description of the Bush and its Inhabitants—The Concert of the Bush—The Tragedians and the Clowns of the Company—The Kangaroo—The Workers and the Idlers of the Bush—Beggars on Horseback.

AUSTRALIA is a vast eucalyptus forest, with a superficial area about equal to that of Europe. Setting aside Queensland, where the vegetation is tropical, the eucalyptus is really the only tree that grows in these regions. In certain parts it attains a prodigious height. I have seen some four hundred feet high, and I measured several that had a circumference equal to that of the famous giants of California. The eucalyptus leaves possess therapeutic properties, which science is engaged in utilizing, and which make Australia one of the most healthy countries of the world. To cure a cold or to keep off mosquitoes it is invaluable. As a disinfectant it is without rival, and every one knows how the marshy parts of south Italy have been made healthy by the introduction of this beneficent tree. There are three kinds of eucalyptus, or gum-tree, found in Australia, commonly called the red, the blue, and the white gum. The red gum is very hard, and is used for house-building and furniture, and for railway sleepers. The white gum is soft, and serves for little except firewood and fences.

From the beginning of April to the end of October

Australia enjoys a magnificent climate, but in January, February, and March the heat is suffocating. The thermometer varies between ninety and one hundred and twenty in the shade, and when the northwest wind blows the atmosphere becomes so frightfully hot that if you were to pass out of it into the infernal regions you would need to take your overcoat with you.

But what a weird, sad-looking landscape! No bright colors. All is dull and sombre, everything seems to be drooping and mourning. The verdure of the soil and of the trees is more gray than green, without any intensity of color, and it never changes in appearance.

The eucalyptus is not a handsome tree. The leaves, which are long and drooping, half close during the day, and give no shade; the trunk peels every year, and the bark hangs down its sides in strips. The numerous branches writhe in despair in all directions. You feel a sentiment of sadness penetrate you at the sight of this vegetation, to which nature has been so niggardly.

Here and there, about the far-stretching landscape, the gum-trees have been burned, or killed by means of an incision around the base of the trunk, and the skeletons are there as in a cemetery, where, on each tomb, you might behold a phantom stretching out a hundred gnarled arms. It is the most lugubrious scene possible. Further on, you come to a clearing, where a thousand gum-trees, gray and dead, appear to be writhing on the ground, and suggest the most fantastic shapes to the mind—twisted serpents, crocodiles lying in wait, gigantic spiders, all sorts of obnoxious creatures on an antediluvian scale.

A little further on the Bush is on fire. Civilized man

is preparing to clear his piece of land. In a few years a prosperous town may have arisen there. For the present it is a scene from the *Inferno*.

With what pleasure you come to a valley, at the bottom of which runs a little rivulet, and where the graceful fronds of the tree ferns surmount warm, brown, scaly trunks of from seven to twelve feet high. The great fronds of two years back hang down round the trunk in golden-brown beauty, while last year's growth forms a dark green umbrella above them. At the summit, rising straight in fresh new green, are the fronds of the year. Australia, so poor in trees, is rich in flowering shrubs, and in the spring the grand crimson blooms of the waratah, and the graceful, golden branches of the wattle do their best to light up and put a little gaiety into this scene of terrible solitude.

And how describe that profound, that solemn silence? I have been told that the Bushman almost loses the faculty of speech in many instances, and it was not at all unusual to hear of shepherds having gone out of their minds. When one thinks of the life these men led— there are fewer employed now—it is not wonderful to hear that their brains gave way occasionally. Miles from any town, unvisited by any human creature save the man who brought him rations from month to month, and whom he missed seeing if he happened not to be in his hut when they were brought, the shepherd was alone in the solemnity of the Bush, his only living companions the thousands of meek sheep and the faithful dog. The cracked scream of the cockatoo and the heartrending note of the crow the only sounds he heard by day; the creepy cry of the morepork and the hoarse croak of the frog the only good-night that ever greeted his ears as he went to rest.

The pall-like silence of the Bush seems to have fallen on even the animals. One never hears the cattle low, and a handful of English sheep being driven to a fresh pasture will make more noise than thousands of Australian ones. You meet them in droves of several thousands, you drive your buggy through the crowd, but you seldom hear a bleat.

However, if you want noise, fire a shot into the trees, and you may chance to disturb a colony of sulphur-crested cockatoos who will raise such a hubbub as will make you instinctively put up your hands to stop your ears. A few moments, and silence reigns once more.

The birds seem to do their best to add to the sadness of the scene. The crow's note is like the cry of a lost soul, a long-drawn, quavering utterance full of anguish. The curlew's shrill and plaintive cry might almost be that of a dying child; but if you want to hear a sound that will sadden your very soul, listen to the morepork at night. Even the liquid and musical babble of the magpies has a tinge of sadness.

Alone, the laughing jackass reminds you that one may find gaiety everywhere, even in the Bush. He laughs consumedly, and his *Hoo-hoo-hoo-hoo, ha-ha-ha-ha* is comic in the highest degree. When you hear him laugh, you want to laugh with him. This smallish, thick-set bird has a head almost as large as his body, and a formidable beak with which he attacks and destroys snakes, so it is not surprising to find that he is held sacred by the law of the Colonies, which forbids you to shoot him.

Justice must be rendered to the frogs that swarm in the Australian marshes, and add their incontestable talent to the concert of the Bush. Some play the raquette with immense spirit and gaiety; others twang the banjo like the cleverest dilettante of Carolina or Florida.

With the exception of the snakes, which swarm, the centipedes, whose bite necessitates the amputation of the bitten member, and a score of other poisonous insects, the Australian Bush contains no savage creatures, none even dangerous.

The kangaroo, the wallaby, the opossum, the chief denizens of the Bush, are all animals with the soft gaze of a gazelle, and perfectly inoffensive; even the little bear of the country, if you take up your gun to shoot it, sits staring up at you, and seems to say, "I have done you no harm; why do you aim that wicked thing at me?"

The wild duck, the hare, the magpie, the paroquet, the love-bird, all these you will find in great numbers in the Bush, besides a host of superbly plumaged birds, among which the lyre-bird, with its tail-feathers forming a perfect lyre-shape, stands preëminent. Besides these, there is a creature impossible to overlook—the hated rabbit, pursued and dreaded more than a wild beast by the Australians, whose pastures he devours. In Europe, if you killed a rabbit without permission, you would lay yourself open to a fine; in Australia, if you aimed at a rabbit and missed it, I believe you would be hanged without a preliminary trial. The hatred is not to be wondered at, for the rabbits make such ravages that squatters go to the expense of putting wire fences all round their immense stations to keep them out. The rabbit race never could have dreamt that it would one day acquire such tremendous importance. More than once the "rabbit question" has occupied the attention of the Parliaments of the different Australasian colonies. The authorities were even for a long while in communication with M. Pasteur, seeking to obtain a virus which might be the means of exterminating the race.*

The most notable Australian creatures are the kangaroo among the quadrupeds, and the emu among the bipeds; the latter is a bird much resembling the ostrich, but is smaller and more thick-set. That gigantic bird, the moa, which was a denizen of the Australasian Bush, can now only be seen in skeleton form in New Zealand museums. Some of them measure sixteen feet in height.

The kangaroo and the emu are still plentiful, but one has to penetrate pretty far into the Bush before one meets with either.

The kangaroo is as mild as a lamb, and never attacks; but when hunted and set upon by dogs, he can defend himself very intelligently. He runs to a spot where he knows there is water. When a dog is too close on him, and he feels there will not be time to find a place of shelter, he goes into the water and waits. The dog follows, and when he is within reach the kangaroo seizes his paws with his own long hind ones, pulls him under water, sits at his ease, and, by means of his short forepaws holds the dog down until death completes the process. It is, as you see, very artistically done.

* A couple of rabbits will, at the end of ten years, have produced a family reaching to the fabulous number of 70,000,000.

If the Australian Bush is melancholy, neither are the figures one meets in its solitudes very gay. The shepherd, or boundary rider, as he is called, is the most important of these, and he is not unpicturesque as he sits loosely on horseback, with limply hanging reins, and wearing a large soft hat, generally inclined over his eyes, to shade them from the brilliant sunshine. His business is to inspect the fences and barriers of a station, and so his days are passed in solitary riding. He —in fact every Bushman—is a splendid rider, although he may not look smart in the saddle. Australian horses are only half broken, and there are hundreds of them that would put the antics of Buffalo Bill's buck-jumpers into the shade.

A sad-looking figure is the "sundowner" who, as his name implies, turns up at sundown and claims the hospitality of the squatter. He is supplied with rations and a shelter for the night. Next morning he goes on his way, if there is no work for him, and directs his steps toward some neighboring station, where he will meet with the same kindness. He is always on the move. Sometimes there is work which he can do, and he stops to earn a few shillings; but more often he is not wanted, and he tramps through the Bush, forgotten, lost, in its immense solitudes. On his back are all his goods and chattels: a blue blanket, and a tin can called a billy, which, with his pipe, generally form his whole *impedimenta*.

As spring advances you meet the more lively figure of the shearer with his two horses, one to carry him, another to carry his baggage. He is seldom alone, but rides in companies of three or four. This man is in comparatively affluent circumstances, since he can earn from one to two pounds a day. The squatter pays a pound for the shearing of each hundred sheep, and there are some shearers so clever at the work that they can shear two hundred a day. When you meet him he is on his way to some station where he has been engaged for the shearing, and he has perhaps twenty or thirty pounds in his pocket. You think, perhaps, that he is going to carry that money to the bank, so as to be able one day to buy a little land and do some farming on his own account. Do not be so sure of it; as likely as not, he will take it to some public-house that he finds on his road, and there he will stay until all the money has gone down his throat. The tavern-keeper is on the look-out for him, and it is he who will be the richer for the man's labor. The shearer, finding his pockets empty, wonders how it is he has no money, and makes up his mind to strike for higher pay next season.

Another figure you will meet, and he, too, is on horseback—always on horseback or driving—is the minister. The good man is going to some squatter's station to pray with the family, who are too far removed from the nearest town to come often to service in church or chapel. He wears a moustache and rabbit-paw whiskers in the Australian fashion, and he is white with dust from head to foot.

Presently it is the doctor you pass, who is perhaps going on a fifty or sixty mile journey through the Bush to attend an urgent case.

Here is the wife of some ordinary farmer. She is returning from the town, where she has been making purchases. She is on horseback, but in ordinary walking dress. Her packages are strapped to the saddle. With her left hand she holds the reins, while with the right she holds a sunshade or umbrella to shelter her from sun or rain.

Everyone you chance to meet in the Bush salutes you, not by inclining the head in the ordinary way, but by a side movement, without any smile or gesture, of the hand.

Everyone rides in Australia—the shop-boy, the postman, the telegraph boy, the lamp-lighter, the beggar even.

I remember having been accosted one day near Musselbrook, by a man on horseback who asked for alms.

"Does that horse belong to you?" I said to him.

"Certainly," he replied. "Why not?"

"I have nothing to say against it," I rejoined, "only I envy you, that is all. I should like to be rich enough to keep a horse of my own like you."

It is true that you can get a horse in the Colonies for a pound or two, and I saw some, not at all bad ones, that had been obtained for a few shillings.

CHAPTER XIII.

The Most Piquant Thing in Australia—Aspect of the Small Towns—Each Takes his Pleasure where he Finds it—Australian Life—Tea, Always Tea—Whiskey or Water—Favorite Occupation—Seven Meals a Day—Squatters.

AUSTRALIA may be divided into two distinct sections; the great towns, that is to say, the capitals of the four principal colonies, Sydney, Melbourne, Adelaide and Brisbane, and about a hundred small towns which, in my eyes, are the real Australia. In the large towns we shall study colonial society; in the small ones we shall see the typical Australian, the pioneer of British civilization.

There is nothing very *piquant* in Australia, unless it be the mosquitoes. Woe betide you if you are a stranger in the land; you will be hailed as a new and succulent dish by these winged anthropophagi. The word will go round, and they will flock from all quarters to taste the newly imported treat. The flies, too, will pester you pitilessly, and follow by thousands in your walks. I have seen men dressed in white coutil literally black from head to waist. A net attached to the brim of your hat, and falling around your head onto your shoulders, will protect your face and neck, and I only hope that the mosquito net will protect you during the night.

All the little Australian towns resemble one another.

One main street, which generally contains the town hall, the post office, the court house, the banks, the hotels, the club and the principal shops, and a few cross streets containing one-storied wooden houses, roofed with corrugated iron. A little removed from the dwelling houses stand the hospital and its garden, neat and admirably kept. Here and there a few churches and chapels represent the different forms of worship that Protestantism has invented. It is good to hear that the followers of the various spiritual guides are all on good terms, and help one another when there is a bazaar to be got up, or work of any kind to be done. I cannot see why they should not still improve on this by all worshiping under one roof. If the town boasts a pretty site—a hill, for instance—and you see a rather important-looking edifice on it, you may be quite sure that it is the Roman Catholic church or a convent. This is infallible.

What strikes you, and first of all astonishes you, is that towns of a thousand to two or three thousand inhabitants should possess so many public buildings. Their town halls and their post offices are often more imposing than those in our towns of fifty or sixty thousand inhabitants. The Bank of New South Wales, which has scores of branches in all the Colonies, including Tasmania and New Zealand, is represented by an edifice, and in some towns by a veritable palace. With the other banks it is much the same. Australia is the land of banks.

The roads in all parts are well cut, well laid, and admirably kept. This strikes the traveler very much, especially any one arriving in Australia from America, where, even in the largest cities, the roads are sometimes rough and dirty as ploughed fields, and one sinks up to the ankle in dust or mud, according to the weather. The Australians have done better still. Almost every little town has its public garden or a park, planted with the different trees of each colony, containing conservatories, well stocked with ferns, palms, and flowers. There are lawns and flower beds, and often a lake with swans and wild ducks on it. The streets are planted with trees on either side; chestnuts, acacias, or gums from the Bush, if the finances of the town do not admit of imported greenery. When I saw some New South Wales towns, Albury, Wagga-Wagga, and others, they were veritable bowers of bloom and verdure. For years past they have been planting three thousand trees a year in Wagga-Wagga.

Each town seeks to outdo its neighbors, and nothing is more amusing than to hear them *tu quoque* one another, but this emulation results in the growth of some very pretty places. Every Australian is persuaded that his town is superior to all the other towns of the Colony, and he is not long in querying whether by chance the axle of the universe will not one day show itself just there. Admire him, he is happy.

Assuredly it is not you, my dear Parisian, who would be able to make yourself happy in the life of a little Australian town. It is not I, either. But I met, in some of these tiny centres of population, rich, very rich people, who said to me, "I am perfectly happy, and if I had a hundred millions I would continue to live here. I do not ask or desire anything better in this world." The out-door life, the freedom, the vastness of the country, all charm them; the chase and athletics form good recreation; agriculture and the breeding of horses, sheep, and cattle, occupy them; they are proud to contemplate the town that they have helped to found where there was once but the wild Bush. They are happy, and it is not to be wondered at.

Nothing breaks the tranquillity of these little towns, unless it be the bi-weekly din of the tambourines and cornets of that gigantic farce called the Salvation Army. If the railway passes through the place, the arrival of the evening train is the event of the day, and a crowd congregates at the station to see it come in.

It is during the wool season that the towns are most full of movement. A loud crack, as of a rifle report, strikes the ear, and there comes into sight along the dusty road a slow-moving wagon, drawn by a team of sixteen or eighteen sturdy, broad-backed oxen, who plod in front of the great load, and look as if no whip or other contrivance of man had power to stir their placid pulses. From six to ten tons of wool are they drawing, perhaps up a steep street, with long, strong, steady pull; at just that gait they set out from their starting-place in the morning, and at just that gait will they go until the moment when they are unyoked at night. Day after day these loads are coming through the town on their way to the railway station, and the sound of the rawhide whips is constantly heard. One grazier has 20,000 sheep to be shorn; another 30,000 or more. Their flocks and herds astonished me, until I had been to Queensland and had heard of a station as large as the whole of England belonging to one man. Even then it was difficult to restrain an exclamation of amazement at the sight of the great mobs of cattle and sheep one is constantly meeting on the road.

For anyone fond of the freedom of an open-air existence, life in the Colonies must be full of charm. Horses are plentiful, so that riding and driving are within the reach of all. Game is also plentiful, and there is no lack of sport for him who loves a gun. The sky is a glorious blue one, and for nine months of the year, if not twelve, the sun invites, nay, entices, to all out-door games. And how all the young Australians respond to the invitation! What picnickings, what tennis tournaments and riding parties, to say nothing of foot-ball and cricket, are always in progress! How many times have I had among my audience at a lecture a party of fifteen or sixteen young people, with perhaps one chaperon, who had driven forty or fifty miles through the Bush to come and hear it; and it was exhilarating merely to see them set off at about ten at night, full of gaiety at the thought of the return home through the moonlit Bush. The rich squatters have splendid teams, and a little business in the chief town of the district is made a pretext for getting up a merry excursion. The four-in-hand is ready, baskets well-filled are put in, and the light-hearted little party drive off. In some suitable spot by the way a halt is made, a champagne lunch is spread and eaten, seasoned with hunger and hilarity. After this pleasant interruption the journey through the Bush is resumed, and the merry party arrive at their destination, ready to do justice to a good dinner at the hotel, and to enjoy any entertainment that may be going on.

For the botanist, for the lover of natural history, what happy hours are in store with the thousand flowers, butterflies and birds of the Bush, and what delight for the artist in the gorgeous sunsets. The sun is leaving the sky, setting in a blaze of crimson and purple and gold that would draw everyone out of doors to see it, if it were not an almost every-day occurrence. But here, in this clear atmosphere, gorgeous sunsets are the rule, and not the exception, so the people of the little Bushtown go on sacrificing to that household god, the teapot, and placidly sup while the sky goes through its marvelous color-harmonies for the benefit of the few stragglers who may happen to be out, and to have eyes to see with. The great disc of fire disappears, and now the sky pales a little; but in ten minutes more comes the afterglow, lovelier than the sunset itself, if possible, and in this half-mysterious light even the little square, iron-roofed houses look almost beautiful. The short twilight soon gives place to night, and the silence of the Bush envelops the town. From far off the barking of a dog, the lowing of a cow, reaches the ear; the crickets chirp, the frogs croak, but nothing stirs; and these sounds do but emphasize the quiet. The men are at their club, the women are at home. Little intellectual activity finding vent in literary societies; no courses of public lectures on science, such as one finds in the veriest villages in America.

The Australians take things easily, and, as a people, are not early risers: at half-past eight plenty of shops are still unopened. They do not walk much: in the afternoon the streets are deserted, even when the atmosphere is delicious and the temperature moderate. As you stroll past the houses you hear the "Maiden's Prayer," or the "Blue Bells of Scotland," being strummed on some old tin-kettle of a piano, and you feel as if you had strayed into some little corner of the England of 1830, pitched down at the antipodes, instead of being in a new community; and this is an impression that will gain strength when you enter the houses and see pictures of racing and hunting, with postilions in high hats, chairs protected by white antimacassars, artificial fruit and flowers under glass shades, and on the mantelpiece terrible things of colored glass with plain glass strips hanging round them, like the dangling front curls of the Englishwomen of that day.

In the hotels the impression will deepen still more. The same bar with the little parlor for the habitués. The walls are covered with the same engravings, boxers and cricketers of days gone by, the eternal "Trial of Charles I.," and the everlasting "Lord William Russell Going to the Scaffold," which in England take the place of our "Death of Poniatowski" or "The Adieux of Napoléon at Fontainebleau."

The English often complain that there is no soap in our hotel bedrooms. There are some who go so far as to conclude that we do not wash. We prefer to use our own soap, which we carry in our trunks with us. Everyone to his taste. In all colonial hotels you find soap. In most you also find a comb and brush. I never saw that brush without saying to myself, "Who spent the night here yesterday? It is enough. I pass," and with a gingerly touch I remove the obtrusive thing.

Just as Æneas carried his household gods from Troy to Italy, so the English have carried their customs from

England to Australia, with this difference, that the gods of Æneas were transferred to a climate like the one they had left, whereas the dry, hot, bracing climate of Australia is the very opposite of the damp, cold, relaxing one of England. It is curious to find the Briton still eating his porridge, even in the tropical parts of Queensland; porridge—a food adopted by the Scotch to keep their blood warm in a cold and humid climate. And there are the same soups, or rather the same soup, Anglo-Saxondom having invented but one as yet; the same roast beef and roast mutton, accompanied by the same potatoes and vegetables, cooked in water, and followed by the same puddings. But I must hasten to say that all these things are well cooked, and not like the nameless horrors served to one in the hotels of little American towns; but, after all, to go to the other end of the world, and be presented with exactly the same fare as in Liverpool or Manchester, is tiresome and disappointing: one would like to see on the bill of fare a dish of kangaroo, a cockatoo *sauté*, or an emu chick *à l'Australienne*. The people one sees in the hotels are nearly all washing down their dinner with water or tea, not from sobriety—for most of the male portion will go to the bar to pass the evening over their whiskey—but from habit. The hotel-keeper does not push his wine, which is dear; he prefers to sell his whiskey, upon which he gets a considerable profit. Australia is now a first-class wine-growing country, and it would have a splendid future in the European markets if the Australians were themselves the first to appreciate their good fortune. As I have already said, the drinkers do not find the wine strong enough in alcohol to please them, and the fanatics preach total abstinence. These latter forget that drunkenness is rarely caused by wine-drinking, and that wine-drinking nations, such as France, Germany, Spain and Italy, are the countries where one finds fewest drunkards.

The Australians pass the greater part of their time at table. At seven they take tea and bread and butter. At half-past eight they breakfast off cold meat, chops or steaks, eggs and bacon and tea. At eleven most of them take a light lunch of beer and biscuit, or tea and bread and butter, according to their sex. At one, or half-past, they dine, and again the teapot is in requisition. At three, afternoon tea is served and swallowed. From six to seven all Australia, broadly speaking, is taking its third meat meal, and again drinking tea. Those who stay up at all late sometimes supplement this with a light collation at ten.

Meat is served at every meal, roast or boiled, and never reappears in the form of appetizing croquettes or stew. Animal food is so cheap (from twopence to fourpence per pound) that *réchauffés* are disdained. As for vegetables, they are boiled in water and served as in England, without any special preparation. Lettuce and celery are constantly eaten without any seasoning but salt. In the matter of cookery, the Anglo-Saxon is about as far advanced as the rabbit.

Most of these little Australian towns are surrounded by immense estates belonging to squatters whose parents acquired them for a few pounds sterling, but which would realize fabulous sums to-day. Very often this is what hinders the towns from going ahead in size and importance. They console themselves with the thought that the squatters keep them going.

A squatter is as proud of his acres as a Duke of Westminster, and he hates to sell any part of his station. His expenses are so far below his income that he would not know what to do with the product of such a sale, and he prefers to keep his land and feel that it is increasing in value.

Perhaps, when the population of Australia increases faster than it does at present, it will be necessary for the Legislators to pass a law to oblige these large holders of land to sell part of their absurdly immense estates at a fixed price, and so allow the country to develop.

But the population will scarcely increase, by immigration, at all events. The Germans, the Swedes, the Norwegians, and the poor Irish, who, together, form the great bulk of European emigrants, go to America or the northwest of Canada. The voyage costs them now less than three pounds, while to go to South Africa or the Australasian Colonies they would need from twelve to eighteen pounds. If an Irish peasant possessed eighteen pounds he would live on his means for the rest of his life.

Population, that is the crying want of Australia.

England too often sends out useless people, family scapegraces, idlers, drunkards, failures of every kind. Australia wants none of these.

What a future Australia would have before her, if she could import from the fields of France those hardy, sober, honest, thrifty laborers, brought up on that old, slow-going soil, in that land of sobriety, common sense, hard work and economy! This is a sentiment that I have often heard expressed by Australians who had seen our field laborers at work.

Unfortunately for Australia, the French peasant does

not emigrate. He loves his country and he stays there.

Mention must be made of the names that those little towns of Australasia have been saddled with. One is named Richmond, another Montpellier, the next Jerusalem. There is a Perth, a Jericho, a Windsor, a Taratatakirikiki, a Berlin, a Canrobert, a St. Arnaud (towns founded at the time of the Crimean war) a Wooroomgorra. A railway station, with three or four little wooden cabins in the background, bears the sounding name of Kensington, the next on the line something that resembles Tararaboomdeay. One of the suburbs of Sydney rejoices in the name of Wooloomooloo. Try and fancy yourself in a civilized country at Wooroomgorra, or Wooloomooloo!

CHAPTER XIV.

The Australian Natives—The Last Tasmanian is in the Museum—A Broken-down King Accepts my Penny—Diana Pays Me a Visit—The Trackers—The Queensland Aborigines—The Boomerang—Curious Rites—The Ladies Refuse to Wash for the Bachelors.

THE Australian aborigines have not given the English much trouble. Humanity has no type more abject or degraded. Possessing neither intelligence nor courage, the race was easily disposed of. Two potions did the work: the Bible, which converted them, and the whiskey-bottle, which diverted them from the care of their territory. New South Wales has very few left, Victoria has still about five hundred, and Tasmania has the skeleton of her last preserved in the museum at Hobart. The type is a horrible one. The body is badly formed, the legs thin, and the arms like those of an orang-outang; the forehead is high, narrow, and receding, the eyes dull; the chin scarcely exists, and is almost merged in the lower jaw, which is receding and very large. The hair is long and fuzzy and looks like a crow's nest.

These savages are the only inhabitants of the earth who have no idea of making habitations for themselves. Three pieces of wood fixed in the ground and supporting the bark of a tree, this is as far as their genius of invention ever led them in the path of architecture.

The unhappy creatures may be met with, straying around the little towns, and rubbing their stomachs to make you understand that they are hungry. If you give them a few pence they go to the public-house. They are the only beggars who will accept copper money; a white would throw it in your face. The native himself begins to have a look of contempt for the penny. One day, when I gave a penny to some black beggar, he looked at the coin, smiled, and said in passable English, "It is a coin of your color I should like, boss, not one of my own." In his time this poor wretch was king of his tribe, I was told, and I gave sixpence to the dethroned sovereign to console him for his lost royalty.

If the men are horrible, the women are revoltingly ugly, with hanging breasts and not a vestige of feminine attractiveness.

One of these creatures—thank Heaven, draped, if not dressed—came one morning to the Western Hotel, Warrnambool (Victoria), and asked to see me.

Diana—it is thus that she is known in this town, where she lives on alms—presented herself at my door hopelessly drunk. She stumbled and muttered a few unintelligible words.

"What do you want?" said I, my hand going to my pocket.

"I have come to pray for you," she said, and thereupon fell on her knees, and began to mutter a prayer.

The sight of this horrible drunken hag, trying to ejaculate a prayer, revolted me, turned me sick. I had meant to give her money, but instead I took her by the arm and put her out.

Diana was scarcely clear of my parlor before she began to swear, calling me by all the names that her vile vocabulary could furnish.

There is another convert for the English to be proud of, I said to myself.

The natives are of no use to the whites. In South

BLACK TRACKER.

Africa amongst them are found workmen of various kinds, and the women make excellent domestic servants. But in Australia King Demos would have something to say to that. Australia belongs to him, and woe betide the Government that would dare to find work for the blacks. They are looked upon as animals and treated as such, although they are no longer killed like wild ones.

When we get to New Zealand, that will be another story; but let us not anticipate.

The sole purpose for which the Government employs the black fellow is to track criminals who have taken refuge in the Bush. At this work they are excellent. They have the instinct of the hound, are soon on the track of a fugitive, and seldom fail to unearth him.

In the north of Queensland you find some of the natives horribly ugly, but vigorous and well built. They are dextrous at the chase, and marvelous is their skill with the boomerang. If ever the Paris Hippodrome were in search of an attraction, the directors would only have to engage a company of North Queenslanders to throw the boomerang and they would be sure to draw all Paris.

The boomerang is a flat piece of wood about two and a half feet long, arched somewhat like a triangle. The Queenslander spies an object at some distance from him. The boomerang, after having hit this object (if it is a living thing its end has come), mounts into the air like a bird, with a whirring as of wings, to a height of sixty to eighty yards, describes immense circles, and, if it was cleverly thrown, comes back in its fall to the feet of the thrower. It is graceful in the highest degree and very marvelous, but do not try your hand at it; it is a dangerous game.

Among the North Queenslanders are tribes who practise rites that are strange and little known. When a male child does not bid fair to be an honor to his race, he is subjected to an operation that shall prevent his

NATIVES OF NORTH QUEENSLAND.
[*From a Photograph by* LOMER & Co., *Brisbane.*]

contributing to the augmentation of the population.

Europe might take a lesson!

The women despise the bachelors. When a man is married, the women are his devoted slaves and proud to wait upon him. "But," said Mr. Meston, the well-known ethnologist of Brisbane, to whom I am indebted for much information on the subject of the natives, "if the man is a bachelor, the women even refuse to wash his clothes for him."

If I only wore the light costume of the Queenslander this would not trouble me. I should not be long doing my own washing.

CHAPTER XV.

Politics and Politicians—The Price of Liberty—The Legislative Chambers—Governors—Comparisons between American and British Institutions—The Politician and the Order of St. Michael and St. George—An Eloquent Candidate—The Honorables—Colonial Peerage—Sir Henry Parkes—A Word to Her Majesty Queen Victoria.

BROUGHT up in the democratic ideas of the mother-country, the Australians, like the English, the French and the Americans, are persuaded that there does not exist among them a man who is not capable and worthy of being Prime Minister, and they are only pitiless toward those who, by their talents or their perseverance, have outshone their fellows. There is not a politician in Australia whom I have not seen dragged in the mire, or spoken of as an incapable man, a schemer, a robber, or, at the very least, a humbug.

Liberty is so great a boon that we can scarcely pay too high a price for it, but one must admit the price is a little exorbitant when the love of equality takes to going hand in hand with a ferocious jealousy of every one who rises above the common level.

Whatever the result may be, the Australian government (I mean the form) is good. This young country manages its own affairs to its own taste. It appoints its own members to the Legislative Assembly or Lower House; it elects the members of the Legislative Council or Upper House.* It not only makes its own laws, levies its own taxes, but it even changes its constitution when it chooses. If the parliaments of the Colonies were to proclaim their independence to-day, a civil war might result, that is to say, a war between Australians and Australians; but it is probable that England would not take part in the quarrel, and that she would accept the decision of the majority or the stronger Australian party.

Australia pays no tribute to England, unless it be the interest of the money England lends her. She has her fleet, her militia, and England sends her neither functionaries nor soldiers. The Governor alone, appointed by the Queen on the recommendation of her Ministers, reminds Australia that she is a branch of the firm, John Bull & Co.

The manager of this branch, then, is supplied by the parent establishment, but he has no more power in the Colonies than the Queen has in England. It is the Ministers, responsible to Parliament, and therefore to the people, who direct his speech and actions; his functions consist in making himself agreeable to the people, calming jealousies, preventing friction between the political parties, or in the relations of the colony with England, but, above all, in gracefully doing the honors of the Government House. He is the leader of colonial society, and for this reason is generally chosen from among the most amiable members of the English aristocracy.

* New South Wales and New Zealand are exceptions. In these two Colonies it is the Governor who appoints the members of the Legislative Council; but he always does it in such a manner as to give satisfaction to the people.

In a word, Australia is a political reproduction of England. Its constitution is built on English lines, and does not resemble the American constitution in the least.

England is a republic with a hereditary president, purely constitutional.

America is an autocracy with an elected monarch, whom the people clothe with a power almost as absolute as that of the Emperor of all the Russias.

In England and in all the English Colonies the Ministers are responsible to the people for their actions.

The Ministers of the United States are only responsible to the President, who appoints them without even giving himself the trouble to make his selection from among the representatives of the people.

If the House of Commons in England declares that the Ministers do not possess its confidence, those Ministers have to retire immediately.

If the Lower House in America makes the same declaration, the Ministers need not take the least notice of it, and they remain in power as long as it pleases the President to retain them.

Neither the Queen of England nor any Governor of her Colonies could take it upon them to appoint or dismiss a mere policeman or custom-house officer.

The President of the United States appoints and dismisses all the servants of the State, from the Ministers down to the postmen, without anyone being able to interfere or object to it.

All this is certainly in favor of the English system; and when the Americans would say to me, " Canada is destined to become part of the United States, and that which will make annexation easy is that the constitution of each American state is the same as that of each Canadian province," I replied, "You are mistaken. The names may be the same, but the things are different. In the two countries the legislative power is democratic, but while the executive power is autocratic in the States, it is democratic in Canada. If the annexation takes place the Canadians will lose by the change."

I have traveled over a great part of the earth's surface; have lived in the two great republics of the world, France and America, and it is my firm conviction that there exists, on this planet, but one people perfectly free, from a political and social point of view, and that is the English.

The form of government in the Colonies leaves them little to be desired, and if only some one could persuade the most capable and the most upright men of good colonial society to look upon it as an honor to represent their countrymen in Parliament, all would go well; but in Australia, as in America, this class of man is apt to hold aloof, and allow the seat, which he ought to occupy, to be filled very often by a noisy demagogue, who has his own and not his country's good at heart, and who takes up three hundred a year if he sits in the Legislative Assembly, and from one thousand to fifteen hundred if he be in the Ministry.

In European democracies, the politician plays on the classes and the masses. In colonial democracies he plays on the loyalty to the mother-country of one part of the community, and national aspirations of the other. Nothing is sadder than to see certain Australian Ministers try to keep their equilibrium and satisfy their ambition in kissing the Queen's hand and cringing before the populace of their own country. At home, the humble servant of the people, whose motto is, "Australia for the Australians;" in the throne-room the courtier whom the Queen is going to make a Knight of St. Michael and St. George, the man loyal to the Crown above all things.

At the Australian Federal Convention held in 1891, the Premier of New South Wales said, "There is an instinct of freedom in Australia which will compel our people at the earliest moment to form a nation of their own." The same man a year later, in England, as a postulant knight, said in public, " I hope the day is far distant when any statesman will endeavor to weaken the cords which bind us to England." The rank democrat had become a democrat of rank, as the witty Sydney *Bulletin* put it.

On returning home, the new-made knight once more posed as the Australian patriot.

Would you like a sample of a certain class of Australian politicians?

The scene passes at an electoral meeting. A candidate makes a violent speech, in which he denounces his opponent in most vehement terms. I will spare you the speech. When the candidate has finished his harangue, one of his partisans rises and proposes a vote of confidence. No one rises to second the proposal. The candidate, indignant, advances to the front of the platform and shouts with stentorian voice " I propose that we adjourn and go and have a drink." Up go all the hands. " I knew every d——d one of you would second that," he exclaimed.

In Australia, as in America, the members of the two legislative houses receive the title of honorable, not only during debates, but in private life. Colonial politicians, when they came to England, used to have themselves announced with their title of honorable. One day the English nobility grew angry at this. They protested, and declared that the "honorable" colonials would have in future to leave their honorableness at the custom-house on landing. Great was the resentment in the Colonies at the news of this affront offered to their representatives. Indignation meetings were forthwith held, and it was resolved that if the English persisted in not recognizing the colonial honorables, the Colonies would refuse in future to recognize English honorables.

In 1853 the Colonies went a little further. On the 28th of July in that year, a Bill was presented in the Sydney Parliament to create a colonial peerage. The good common sense of the Australian people soon disposed of this huge joke. However, it would have been droll to hear announced in the drawing-rooms of the old English aristocracy the Duke and Duchess of Wooloomooloo, the Marquis and Marchioness of Parramatta and the Earl and Countess of Cockatoo Island.

Among the politicians of the Colonies there are a few who have raised themselves above the ordinary level, and who merit the name of statesmen. Of such are the late Sir John Macdonald, Premier of Canada, Sir Henry Parkes, Premier of New South Wales, now in his 79th year, and Mr. Cecil Rhodes, Premier of Cape Colony, who may be called the uncrowned king of South Africa, and of whom I shall speak later.

Sir Henry Parkes is a most interesting personality.

It is impossible to forget him: an enormous head covered with a forest of white hair, a shrewd and penetrating glance, a slow and unctuous voice; an inimitable mixture of the lamb and the fox. Sir Henry Parkes is the champion of fiscal liberty and Australasian unity. His pet dream is to see the seven colonies of Australasia set aside their ridiculous jealousies and make one family.

There are four immense provinces in the north of America which form but one Canada, and are all the better for it; why should not the seven Australasian colonies combine themselves into one powerful confederation? But such are the jealousies that, to appease in advance those of Melbourne and Sydney, it has already been resolved that, if ever Australian confederation comes to pass, it shall be Albury, a little town of three thousand inhabitants, situated on the frontier of Victoria and New South Wales, that shall be made the capital of Australia. It is already dubbed the Federal City.

Sir Henry Parkes will die without seeing his dream realized. It is not confederation that the people of the Colonies demand, but still more separation. Queensland at this very time is moving heaven and earth to get divided into two colonies; there are even to be found Queenslanders who go so far as to ask that their colony be split up into three.

During a short stay at Rockhampton I received a deputation of notables who came to talk of their grievances, and pushed childishness so far as to ask me to promise that, on returning to Europe, I would use all my influence to get the colony of Queensland separated into two independent parts.

I received these gentlemen with all the seriousness of which I am capable, and I promised. Now I have kept my word, for how can I doubt that the Queen of England and the Ministers of Her Britannic Majesty will read my book and accede to the righteous demands of the worthy Queensland patriots?

My commission is, therefore, executed.

CHAPTER XVI.

The Resources of Australia—The Mines—2,500 Per Cent. Dividends—Wool—Viticulture—The Wealth of Australia Compared to the Wealth of Most Other Countries—Why France is Richer than Other Nations.

AUSTRALIA is a vast continent, equal to four-fifths of the superficial area of Europe. It contains a tract of sterile land here and there; but, roughly speaking, its bowels are full of precious ore, and its surface is admirably suited for raising cattle, grazing sheep, and growing corn and fruit. If Australia had better rivers it would be another America; unfortunately, it lacks water and hands; its rivers in summer are mostly trickling streams or empty ditches, and the hands are not there to overcome the difficulty by irrigating the land.

Up to the present day, gold, silver and wool have been the principal products of Australia.

The town of Bendigo produced in a few years £65,000,000. Ballarat ran this performance very close. Broken Hill produces 300,000 ounces of gold per week. Mount Morgan, in Queensland, is a mountain of gold. To get at the precious metal, the miners only have to cut into the mountain, as one would cut a slice of cake.

Needless to talk of the fabulous fortunes that have been made in a few days.

When Broken Hill was discovered nine years ago, a company was formed, and shares were issued at £1.

What was the history of those shares? Here is a short and authentic story, which will show you:

A merchant in Adelaide bought a hundred of these shares, and presented them to his wife. " Take them, my dear," he said ; " I rather fear it may be one hundred pounds thrown away; but who knows? The affair may prosper, perhaps, and if dividends should come, you will be so much in pocket." He had just retired from business. After having sold his concern, he went to England, intending to live there on his income. On landing in London, he learned that the bank in which he had placed his capital had failed. Not only had he lost the value of his shares, but, as a shareholder, he was called upon to pay a sum which swallowed up every penny he possessed. He was still young. He determined to return to business, and, without unpacking his trunks, started for Australia again. On arriving at Adelaide he found that the Broken Hill shares that he had bought at £1 were worth £480 apiece. Thus his wife, to whom he had given a hundred one-pound shares, was worth £48,000. He realized this fortune, invested it in Government consols, and does not blush to live on his wife's income.

The Mount Morgan gold mine has produced results just as fabulous. The histories of Bendigo and of Ballarat abound in anecdotes of the same nature, and South Africa has more wonderful ones still. However, if I may offer you advice, buy three-per-cents. guaranteed by the State; there has been more money thrown into mines than has ever been taken out of them.

For this reason the Australians do not count upon their mines for a living. It is their sheep, the fleeces of which find a ready sale in all the markets of the world, that form the wealth of Australia.

Viticulture is making enormous progress. The Australian wines, surcharged with alcohol, as they generally are, very much resemble our Roussillon wines. They are lacking in delicacy; but the wine-growers are beginning to understand that the wine-making art, which has been perfected in France by centuries of experimental study, is not to be learned in a day, and one after another they have been sending to France for experts, whom they have placed at the head of their vineyards.

Up to now little Australian wine has been consumed in the Colonies. The water-drinkers, the fanatics of all shades, preach temperance (a word which in English signifies total abstinence, and not moderation), the Governments put on an enormous duty;* the hotel-keepers charge three to six shillings a bottle for the most ordinary kinds, and the result is, that the bulk of the people drink water, tea or whiskey, and the rich drink the wines of France and Germany.

As yet, Australia does not produce a thirtieth part of the wine consumed by London alone. I predict that in twenty years Australia will be sending her wines to the four corners of the world. When all the other inhabitants of the globe are drinking it, perhaps the Australians may make up their minds to taste what it is like.

The private wealth of America is £39.0.0 per inhabitant; of England, £35.4.0; of France, £25.14.0; of

* The duty on a three-shilling bottle of wine entering Victoria from New South Wales, or *vice-versâ*, is three shillings.

Germany, £18.14.0; of Austria, £16.6.0. The private wealth of Australia is £48.

Then the Australian is the richest man in the world. Not at all.

If two people living together possess, one £8,000 and the other nothing, they possess, say statistics, £4,000 each. This ought to be a great comfort to number two. Australia, like America and England, has some very wealthy men, squatters and mine-owners, who, in a few years, have amassed millions, and in the large towns she has a population of more than a hundred thousand people, for whom, each morning, existence is a problem hard to solve.

England and America are the countries where fortunes are most disproportionate. On one hand millionaires living in unbridled luxury; on the other, poor starving wretches huddled together in frightful hovels, in a state of numb despair induced by overwhelming evils.

England and America are also the two countries where people speculate the most. Now, it is not speculation that enriches a country, it is production. Speculation enriches a few individuals at the expense of a few others. The money passes from one pocket to another in this way, without the country having benefited by the transaction. The products of the soil and of industry are the only sources of real riches in a country. Speculators are the country's enemies, encouraging a man to make a gain which shall be another man's loss. When the great day of social reform arrives, which is coming with giant strides, we shall see, I hope, the extermination of the speculator. Everything has a real value, and I fail to see why stocks should attain a high fictitious value by the manœuverings of a few speculators. Perhaps I am very obtuse, but I never can see why consols should vary because a sovereign or a statesman makes a speech more or less amiable. By work I have earned and put by one hundred pounds, which I lend to the Government on condition that it pays me three pounds a year: for the life of me I cannot see why these hundred pounds should only be worth ninety-eight pounds, because the King of Italy has a cold in his head, or the Emperor of Germany a fit of indigestion, or why they should be worth a hundred and two pounds, because the Emperor of Russia has sent New Year's greetings to the Sultan of Turkey. These are things which are beyond my comprehension.

Speculators were unknown a hundred and fifty years ago. When will they disappear from the face of the earth?

It is they who are the cause of the commercial and financial crises, which bring America and Australia within a hair's-breadth of bankruptcy every few years.

Australia is overrun with speculators and bookmakers, she who ought to have only farmers, manufacturers, traders, mechanics and laborers. The bookmakers make as much as £20,000 a year, and every year hundreds of individuals go there from England, hoping to live by speculations in mines and horse-racing.

I can wish nothing better to Australia than that she may soon be able to sweep her territory of all such parasites.

The day she has the courage to send the surplus population of her towns to fell the Bush forests; the day she has succeeded in learning that there is but one means of growing rich, for nation or for individual, and that is by work and thrift; the day she ceases to try and enrich herself by unhealthy speculation, Australia will see her credit firmly established. Disproportions will melt away, and with them all poverty; the population will increase, and the riches of the country, drawn from regular work, will become stable.

It is the stability of fortunes, and a seemly distribution of wealth that makes a country really rich, and not a few colossal fortunes collected in a few pockets. Three-quarters of the land in England is in the hands of about thirty families. In France, at the present day, more than six millions of people are land-owners, and more than half the people are the owners of the houses they inhabit. This is why France is the richest nation in the world. It is she who has the most masters and men working on their own account. It is she alone who, thanks to the order and economy which reigns in the *bourgeoisie*—the shop-keeping class and the peasantry—can pass through a commercial crisis and lend money to a foreign government.

The land was never intended to support three persons: a landlord, a tenant, and a laborer. Jacques Bonhomme is in himself a landlord, tenant and laborer, that is why he prospers. His wife does not follow the fashions nor go in for the high-hand shake. She rises at four or five o'clock in the morning, feeds her own poultry, and that is why they look so well.

All nations, the new countries especially, envy France her economical and laborious rural population. And well they may; it is Jacques Bonhomme and his good wife who are the fortune of France.

CHAPTER XVII.

The Workman Sovereign Master of Australia—His Character—The Artist and the Bungler—A Sham Democrat—Government by and for the Workingman—Public Orators—Stories of Workmen—End of the Tragic Story of a Russian Traveler.

THE sovereign ruler of Australia is neither the Queen of England, nor the Governor appointed by her, nor the Parliament, nor the Ministers chosen in that Parliament; the sovereign ruler of Australia is the workingman.

If this personage were but content with his lot, and the country prospered under his rule, there would be little to be said against this arrangement; but, unhappily, he does not turn to account the inexhaustible resources that nature has placed in his reach on this immense continent, and he takes good care that no one else shall profit by them. The Australian workman, still less interesting than his English cousin and *confrère*, is lazy, fond of drink, a devoted keeper of Saint Monday, a spendthrift who thinks only of his pleasures and takes no interest whatever in the development of his country. He will throw up the most lucrative job to go and see a horse-race a hundred miles from his home. His labor is purely mercenary, a task got through anyhow. He has served no apprenticeship worth the name, received no technical instruction. He is by turns carpenter, locksmith, mason, gardener, vine grower, carter, shearer, and, at a push, schoolmaster.

He strikes frequently, but it is not in order to try and earn more, so that out of his savings he may set up in trade or farming. No, he wants to gain more in order to be able to spend more. He has no pride in his work, no jealousy about its quality. He takes up enormous wages, which he spends in frivolity, and at the end of the year finds himself just where he was before. A French gardener is a botanist; a French cabinet-maker is an artist. The mass of Anglo-Saxon workmen are bunglers, and have not the least artistic instinct in them. It is not altogether their fault. There are few or no technical schools for them on week days, and no art museums open on Sundays. The Pecksniffs, the Podsnaps, the Chadbands and all the Tartufes of their native land prevent their making acquaintance with the works of art that might elevate them; they know only sensual pleasures, and when they have filled themselves with gin or whiskey they declare they have enjoyed themselves.

It is the money he saves, and not the money he earns, which enriches a man. This is a truism which the Anglo-Saxon workman has not yet discovered.

At Broken Hill, the place which produces more silver than any other in the world, I had the following conversation with a miner who was out on strike:

"The mines ought to be nationalized and to belong to the people," he said. "Look at me; what do I earn? Three pounds a week! Yet *I* go down into the mines to fetch the silver; *I* do the work. Three pounds a week! What is a man to do with three pounds a week?"

The miner on strike was a bachelor.

"Since you ask me, I will tell you what a man can

do with three pounds a week," I replied. "You are away here in a desert; distractions are few. You are young. Work for a couple of years. Spend twenty shillings a week and put by the other forty. In one year's time you will have a hundred pounds saved; at the end of two years you will have more than two hundred. You talk of nationalizing the mines. Let the five thousand miners who are employed here follow the advice I have given to you, and in two years you might between you buy all the shares, and the mine would be yours. If you have not confidence in the mine, do not be jealous of the shareholders. Buy land, cultivate it or run sheep on it, and you are land-owners at once."

If I had talked Hebrew to the fellow, he could not have looked at me more blankly.

"Ah!" he exclaimed, "leave me alone. You are no democrat; you are no friend of the people."

"I beg your pardon," I returned; "I am a thorough democrat. The man who has not the self-control to impose a few privations on himself, and put by something, inspires not the slightest sympathy in me. The man who, by his own fault, possesses nothing is a slave. I call a democrat the man who is independent and his own master. The middle classes have become a power because they have known how to save money. I would not have the workingman be a slave, I would have him possess something; but he will only be in that position when he has learned to deny himself and put something in reserve. In Europe, the workman very often does not get the wages he deserves, and he is right to raise his voice in these cases; but in Australia it is his fault if at the end of a few years he is not independent."

My miner had already turned his back.

I am ready to acknowledge that the times are changed, and that before long every worker will exact from labor independence and an honorable place in society ; but if the future belongs, and reasonably, too, to the worker, it is certain that it will never belong to the lazy or the thriftless.

In a country where the Government sells land at five shillings an acre, payable in ten years, I maintain that every man who has a few pounds in his pocket can easily acquire independence, and will long be able to, since Australia proper has scarcely more than three million inhabitants, and the continent is large enough to accommodate a population of more than fifty millions.

The government of Australia by the workingman for the workingman is sublimely ridiculous. These Australian workmen who, for the most part, have come to Australia at the expense of English emigration societies, are the same men who have forced the Government to stop emigration. There are no more wanted. Australia belongs to them. And what do they do? They vegetate in Sydney and Melbourne, and the country cries aloud for hands to cultivate it. The hands are in the cities, with their arms folded, loafing about the public-houses and street-corners. The squatters are obliged to use their land in grazing cattle and sheep, which there is often no market for, because one man can look after thousands of sheep, but agriculture demands many laborers. If Australia were peopled with intelligent and hard-working cultivators of the soil, it might be the granary of the universe. Here and there you see a flourishing farm which has been made and developed in a few years. You find it belongs to a German or a Swede. Near the towns you constantly see kitchen-gardens in a high state of cultivation. Not an inch of the ground is wasted. In a corner of this garden is a hut occupied by the patient, hard-working Chinaman, whom the Australian despises, but whom he would do much better to imitate. The Chinaman is sober, minds his own business and gets up no strikes; he goes on his jog-trot way; he owns a horse and a little cart, and every year sends home to his country the money that he has saved by sheer hard labor.

Meanwhile the workman of Sydney goes to Hyde Park to listen to the inanities, the balderdash given off by a lot of ragged wind-bags, professional loafers, parasites whom the new communities of the far west of America would chase ignominiously from their midst. And what harangues! I remember one great fellow with a low forehead and an immense mouth, with nonchalant gestures and a drunkard's voice, a ne'er-do-weel of the worst type, who bawled forth a discourse on *Authoritatism*.

The crowd stood around open-mouthed and staring their eyes out with trying to understand. The conceited idiot was so proud of the word that his mouth was full of it, and he repeated it at every instant. Presently one of the crowd politely asked the orator to spell the word and explain what it meant; he was ignominiously expelled from the circle.

"*Authoritatism,*" cried the ranter, "that is the source of all the mischief. Strikes are the only remedy." And as those who were listening to him had already all struck, and thus killed the goose that laid the golden eggs, he advised them to devour what remained, namely the goose.

If a loafer like this made a speech of that kind in Texas, Colorado, or any of the Western States, the population, not the authorities, would give him twenty-four hours to find some honest employment or quit. If at the end of twenty-four hours he had done neither the one nor the other, he would run the risk of seeing himself suddenly promoted to an elevated position—at the top of a tree. Western America is a hive of bees, and no drones are allowed to establish themselves there to create disorder and preach laziness.

The workman is loud in his demand for coöperation. But is it he who invents machines or buys them? Is it he who risks his money in enterprises which may or may not succeed? He is willing to share the profits, but he is not willing to run the risks. He demands that disputes between capital and labor be settled by arbitration. Very good; but, suppose that the arbitrators give a case against him, he goes straightway to his companions and cries, "I have lost, and you call that arbitration, do you?"

Oh, the number of stories of workmen that were told me in Australia!

A journeyman-gardener, who had long been out of work, presented himself at the house of a Melbournian, and asked for employment.

"I have nothing to give you to do just now; however, since you are in want, you may tidy my garden."

A few hours would have amply sufficed for the work. The man spent two days raking the garden, and clipping a few trees, which did not need touching.

This being done, the Melbournian, who had employed the man out of pure charity, handed him twelve shillings. " What's that? " cried the workman, indignantly. " Don't you know that a gardener's pay is seven and sixpence a day, and not six shillings? You are trying to take advantage of my misfortune. I do not work for less than seven and sixpence a day."

The Melbournian vowed, but a little late, that he would not be caught again.

The Australian squatter is at the mercy of the laborers and shearers he employs. Some of these gentry do not even recognize themselves as bound by a contract. A vine-grower had engaged twenty workmen to proceed with his grape harvest. When the grapes were gathered, the workmen said to their employer: " Now, we want ten shillings a day instead of eight. If you do not give us these terms, we shall leave off work to-day, and let your grapes rot on the ground." The land-owner ploughed up his vines in disgust, and this is not a solitary case by any means. Where the vines flourished a few sheep are now grazing.

Meanwhile the workman loafs about the large towns, and listens to harangues on the tyranny of the squatter.

Maid-servants earn from four to six pounds a month, yet for the least trifle they leave their situations, and complain of ill-usage. The only remedy for the evil would be the reëstablishment of polygamy. An Australian wife, like the wife of the Zulu, would say to her husband, " Really, John, I have too much on my hands, it is time you married another housemaid."

Alas, one hears of evils everywhere, but of very few remedies. Each has his program of destruction, but no one has a program of construction. I think we are very near the end of our patience.

A well-known socialist, at a public banquet, was comparing the modern workman to the wolves in the famous Russian story.

"Yes," said he, "the man was in a sleigh with his wife and his children. Soon they were pursued by hungry wolves. To appease them the man threw them his provisions. The wolves seized the provisions and devoured them, and then they joined together again in their pursuit of the traveler. He threw them one child, then another, then his wife. But still the wolves pursued, and devoured the man and the horses. Well, gentlemen, the workingmen accept your concessions, but I am too honest not to tell you that these concessions will not satisfy them. They will demand again, and continue to demand until they have obtained everything."

He laid great stress upon *everything*.

In other words, the man of the middle class has been a tyrant, and now it is the workingman who is going to tyrannize in his turn.

The socialist in question had related the story of the Russian traveler very well. But he might have ended it. I will end it for him:

It is true that the wolves devoured the traveler's provisions, his children, and his wife, also that they devoured him and his horses. But they did not stop there. They wanted to begin again next day, but at the turn of a road they met with a hundred armed men, who put an end to their insatiable pretensions.

CHAPTER XVIII.

The Religions of the Colonies—The Catholic Church and its Work—The Baptists and the Sweet Shops—Good News for the Little Ones—A Presbyterian Landlady in Difficulties—I Give a Presbyterian Minister his Deserts—Christian Association of Good Young Men—The Big Drum or the Church at the Fair—Pious Bankers—An Edifying Prayer.

ACCORDING to the latest statistics published with authority of the Government, this is how Australia stands with regard to the religions professed by the inhabitants :

Anglicans,	39.10
Catholics,	21.10
Presbyterians,	13.
Wesleyan Methodists,	9.50
Primitive Methodists,	1.60
Other Methodists,	0.30
Congregationalists,	2.10
Baptists,	2.30
Lutherans,	2.
Salvationists,	1.10
Jews,	0.40
Buddhists, Mohammedans, etc.,	1.20
Other religions, that is to say, the hundred and one other dissenting sects,	4.20
Persons who refused to say to what religion they belonged,	2.10

In New South Wales, the population of which colony is 1,130,216, the numbers are as follows:

Anglicans,	509,283
Catholics,	286,915
Presbyterians,	109,383
Wesleyan Methodists,	97,487
Primitive Methodists,	20,352
Other Methodists,	2,269
Congregationalists,	24,112
Baptists,	13,102
Lutherans,	7,904
Salvationists,	10,312
Jews,	5,484
Buddhists, Mohammedans,	10,790
Other religions,	28,730
Religion unknown,	14,093
Total,	1,130,216

One cannot but be struck, on reading this list, by the progress made and the importance acquired by the Catholic religion in the English Colonies. This importance had also struck me in Canada, the United States, and the Pacific Islands. And yet, there is nothing astonishing about it, when one thinks how easy it must have been for those charitable and devoted priests, who consecrate soul and body to the service of the poor and unhappy, and to the education and placing out of their children, to win converts among the struggling colonists, hungry for sympathy, and always ready to open their hearts to those who lead, like themselves, a life of privations and sacrifices. The life of these priests is so exemplary, that Australians of all creeds speak of them with the greatest respect, and when they indulge in criticisms or jokes on the clergy, it is never at the expense of a Catholic priest.

The clergy of the Anglican church, that aristocratic and worldly institution, do not attract the masses. As a rule, they themselves seek the best society.

The pastors of the hundred and eighty and odd dissenting churches rival one another in angular and intolerant piety, expending their energies in disputing over the interpretation of certain passages of Scripture, enemies of the most innocent gaiety, business men on the look-out for an income to maintain a family, often large; how could such men compete for the affection and respect of the masses with the Catholic priests, full of the naïve gaiety, the innocent good humor, and the simple candor which are so often found in people who pass their lives in contributing to the happiness of others, and in leading a life of complete self-abnegation and untiring devotion.

But if the Catholic Church in the Colonies inspires a French visitor with nothing but respect and admiration, and the English Church with sentiments of respect and indifference, all the little dissenting sects furnish ample materials for edification and amusement.

On the 2d of June, 1892, I read the following in the Melbourne *Argus*:

"The opening of fruit and confectionery shops on Sunday, at which children spend the money given them by their parents to put in the missionary boxes at Sunday-school, was brought under the notice of the half-yearly session of the Baptist Association of Victoria yesterday by the Rev. Edward Isaac, who moved: 'That this

Association views with the deepest regret the way the missionary money, given to the Sunday-school children by the parents for a specific purpose, is so largely diverted from the proper channel, owing to the Sunday opening of fruit and confectionery shops. Further, that this Association would, with all earnestness, respectfully urge the remedying of this crying evil (*sic*) upon the attention of the Government, by passing a statute making the closing of the aforesaid shops compulsory between the hours of two and four o'clock on Sunday afternoon.' The resolution was seconded, and carried unanimously."

This is protection with a vengeance.

In the same paper was the report of a Chinaman having been condemned to pay a fine of half a crown for having worked in his kitchen garden on Sunday. In order to condemn him, the magistrate had had to unearth an old unrepealed edict made in the days of Charles II., the Merry Monarch of burlesque reputation.

During my sojourn in Canada, a butcher of Montreal was condemned to pay a fine of eight dollars for not having knelt during divine service. It appeared that the poor fellow suffered from rheumatism; but this did not exempt him in the eyes of his judge.

Would you not think we were living in the days of the Inquisition instead of in the end of the nineteenth century? After this, can you ask whether the Colonies are progressionist countries?

The best is yet to tell.

A few days before leaving Canada, I saw in the papers that the Presbyterians had assembled in solemn conclave to expunge from their profession of faith the article on infant damnation. The motion was carried in spite of violent opposition. Poor dear little babies—whom the old article of the Presbyterian faith made it so hot for—rejoice, for you have been accorded a chance to reform.

I am not responsible for the following, which was told me—not by a Presbyterian.

The keeper of a lodging-house, a lady with very decided Presbyterian views, only opened her house to those whose orthodoxy was as unquestionable as her own. However, business flagged somewhat, the house was half empty, and she pondered over many things. "Perhaps business would mend if I relaxed my views a little," she said to herself.

One day an old gentleman presents himself at the door, looks at the apartments, and makes choice of some rooms.

" Excuse me," says the landlady ; " before anything is decided, I must know whether you are a strict Presbyterian ? "

" I scarcely understand what you mean," replied the worthy man.

" Well, for instance, do you believe that all children who die unbaptized will be eternally burnt ? "

" Upon my word," says the new lodger, his memory perhaps alighting upon some unruly little imp of his acquaintance, " I should scarcely like to say *all*, but some will, no doubt."

" I will let you the rooms," replied the good woman ; "*some* is scarcely to my liking, but at all events that is better than none."

And now let us take a taste of Presbyterianism in a New Zealand town.

I had just returned to the hotel after having given a lecture on the Scotch, at the Town-hall. I was half undressed, when there came a knock at my bedroom door. It was a waiter bearing a card; the Presbyterian minister of the town wished to see me at once on a very urgent matter. I bid the waiter show the reverend gentleman up.

A man of about fifty, in the usual black ecclesiastical coat and white cravat, and holding a soft felt hat, appeared in the doorway, wearing a sad face.

I recognized him at once as one of my audience that evening. For a whole hour and a half I had vainly tried to make him smile. He was on the first row. Those wet blankets always are.

"Excuse my costume," I began; "but you wished to speak to me on urgent business, and I thought best not to make you wait."

"There is nothing the matter with your dress," he broke in; "this is not an affair of the body, but of the soul. I have come to pray for you; allow me to kneel."

I was taken a little by surprise, and felt a trifle discountenanced, but I quickly regained composure.

"Why, certainly," I said; "with the greatest pleasure, if it can make you happy."

He knelt, put his elbows on the bed, buried his head in his hands, and began—

"Lord, this man whom Thou seest near me is not a sinful man; he is suffering from the evil of the century; he has not been touched by Thy grace; he is a stranger, come from a country where religion is turned to ridicule.

Grant that his travels through our godly lands may bring him into the narrow way that leads to everlasting life."

The prayer, most of which I spare you, lasted at least ten minutes.

When he had finished my visitor rose and held out his hand.

I shook it.

"And now," said I, "allow me to pray for you in my turn."

He signified consent by a movement of the hand.

I did not go on my knees, but with all the fervor that is in me, I cried—

"Lord, this man whom Thou seest beside me is not a sinful man. Have mercy upon him, for he is a Pharisee, who doubts not for one moment, and that without knowing me, that he is better than I. Thou who hast sent in vain Thy Son on earth to cast out the Pharisees, let Thy grace descend upon this one; teach him that the foremost Christian virtue is charity, and that the greatest charity is that which teaches us that we are no better than our brethren. This man is blinded by pride; convince him, open his eyes, pity him and forgive him, even as I also forgive him. Amen."

I looked at my good Presbyterian. He was rooted to the floor, amazement written on his face.

I once more took his hand and shook it.

"And now," said I, "we are quits. Good night."

He went away somewhat abashed, pocketing the mild reproof as modestly as he could.

Here, again, is something in the same line which is not unedifying:

In the month of May, 1892, I gave fourteen lectures

at the Centenary Hall in Sydney, a very pretty hall belonging to a Wesleyan Society, who had let it to us for the purpose. I shall never forget the reception that the Sydney people gave me in that hall. Never did I address a warmer, more intelligent, or more sympathetic audience. In October of the same year I returned to Sydney, on the very day that France lost the greatest prose writer of the century, Ernest Renan. I had known the illustrious writer; more than once had he given me the benefit of his counsel, more than once had he cheered me with encouraging words.* I was asked to give a lecture on him. To speak the eulogy of Renan, to talk of his life and his work to the people of Sydney, this appeared to me an opportunity of paying a debt of gratitude to the memory of this man of genius. I accepted with joy. My manager again hired the Centenary Hall; the public filled it in every part, and the press next day joined its applause to that of the public.

The lecture was such a success, that I was requested to repeat it, and again I agreed with alacrity. But alas! this lecture had not satisfied every one, and we had raised the most terrible and the most unforgiving of all wraths—the wrath of the bigots.

A member of the Young Men's Christian Association of Sydney went to the secretary of the Centenary Hall, and represented the danger that the reputation of the Wesleyan Society was running in allowing the hall to

*It was Renan who had made me happy one day, by saying to me, "I have read your *John Bull et son Ile*, and although I laughed heartily at the eccentricities that you describe, your volume has made me love the English better."

be used for giving a panegyric on Renan, an "atheist," the author of the *Vie de Jésus*. This amiable person had (it may be said in parenthesis) received a free pass to all my lectures.

The secretary of the Centenary Hall thought it his duty to protest. Thanks be, my manager held him to his engagement, and the lecture on Renan was repeated with all the success that had attended its first delivery.

Ah, heaven knows how I myself would have liked to protest against having to speak of Ernest Renan, that giant of grace and power, in a hall devoted twice a week to the worship rendered by a sect who have narrowed the Divinity, the Incomprehensible, down to their comprehension.

What did Renan demand all his life long, if it was not the liberty to compose for himself the romance of the infinite, and the liberty to discuss every religious question? Is not this Protestantism in its very essence? The intolerance of certain dissenters is veritably epic. Here are people who exist simply because their ancestors in days gone by combated for liberty of conscience, but who, now that the battle is won, have become intolerant even to the point of refusing to others that liberty to think, to act, and to discuss—in fact, the liberty to which they themselves owe their existence.

And, setting aside the religious question, was there ever a man who lived a purer life than that of Renan, more perfectly consecrated to the search after truth and the amelioration of the human race?

But what did they know of Renan, these narrow Christians, and the good young man who, after having accepted favors from my manager, played him this trick of a sneak behind his back?

The intolerance of these people is beyond conception. When I arrived at Maitland, a rather important town in New South Wales, the Mayor and the Town Council were kind enough to give me a welcome in the Town-hall, and drink my health in a glass of champagne. Among the townspeople who had accepted an invitation to the little gathering, was the vicar of the chief church, a charming, genial man.

Next day several dissenters of the town (I do not remember whether they were Wesleyans, Socinians, Baptists, Lutherans, Presbyterians, Swedenborgians, Plymouth Brethren, very certainly they were not Christians), several dissenters, I say, attacked the vicar, with all the energy of bigots, "for having taken part in a reception given in honor of a man whose lectures were announced in the papers under the name of *Comedy Lectures*" (*sic*).

"Ah," said an Australian, "unco guid," to me one day, with a deep sigh, "you French do not pass the Sunday in prayer as we do."

"No," I replied; "in France we have not to pass every seventh day in repenting of what we have done during the other six. Take that!"

And now, for the final touch, allow me to reproduce here the advertisement of a sermon which I extracted from the advertisement column of a New Zealand paper.

"*In response to numerous requests,*
the Rev. Pastor B. will, on Sunday next, deliver a sermon on the Vanity of Life's Pleasures."

There were elaborate instructions about reserved seats, and entrance by side-doors. Then followed a synopsis of the performance, which read very much like a Surrey-side play-bill—

1. "The Pulpit Upset!"
2. "Deliver or Die!"
3. "God in the Mansion House!"
4. "Running his Horse for the Cup."
5. "What! Dear Lord, have you come for me?"
6. "The Corpse on the Bed."
7. "*The Good Angel at the Lamp-post!*"
8. "*Seen in a Dancing-room.*"
9. "Nothing but what I stand in."
10. "A Cannibal Song will be sung by the Tabernacle Choir."

. . The line, *Nothing but what I stand in*, suggested the idea of a young Maori girl attired in a few cowrie beads, for in parenthesis was added, "Very delicate business."

It was a brilliant idea to terminate the performance with a cannibal song by the Tabernacle choir.

Bang-bang, beat the big drum, walk up, ladies and gentlemen.

The Rev. Pastor in question was good enough to send me a ticket.

He thought to do me a politeness, no doubt. May heaven reward him!

Under the heading of *Signs of the Times*, I read the following paragraph in the Sydney *Methodist Gazette:*—"There has been formed in our town a Bankers' Christian Association, the president of which, a Methodist minister, was formerly a bank manager.

The directors, managers, and clerks meet together twice a week for prayer and the study of the Bible. One of the principal banks of Sydney is so well known for the piety of its directors and *employés*, that it is often mentioned under the name of the Christian Bank."

And the week after, the incorrigible *Bulletin* had the following in its own characteristic style :

"'A sign of the times!' Yes! Also, it is characteristic of the average 'follower' that his cash won't square, and that he goes away the night before the audit. The BULLETIN doesn't want to make any trouble at present, so it refrains from giving the name of the bank, but some day, perhaps, this paper will point out the institution in question, and then there will be a mad rush of depositors, and the management will have to heave the earnest followers down the front steps to pacify the raging mob."

The fact is that the "Christian" banker is celebrated for directing his eyes towards heaven and his steps towards the frontier.

Poor Australian bankers! A fortnight after I left Australia, more than half the colonial banks failed one after another. Never did such a panic seize the financial world. A crash had been long foreseen ; but the most pessimistic of the prophets of evil scarcely expected a collapse so rapid.

Among Anglo-Saxons the most tragic scenes are generally accompanied by very comic ones. As in Shakespeare, the sublime and the ridiculous, tragedy and farce, go hand in hand.

It was the Anglican Bishop of Sydney, Protestant Primate of Australia, who took it upon him to strike the comic note. Every one knows that in a time of public calamity, in England or the Colonies, it is incumbent upon the Primate to compose a special prayer for the use of the faithful, a prayer to appease the wrath of heaven. The Common Prayer-Book contains, it is true, an endless number of special prayers, for rain, for fine weather, for peace, for the harvest, etc.; but the men who put these together did not foresee such things as financial panics, and the Bishop of Sydney had to compose something new and suitable for the occasion.

Here is the prayer that he evolved, and which was used in the church and in the family, in the year of grace 1893, that is to say, at the end of the nineteenth century—

"O Almighty God, whose righteous providence ordereth all things in heaven and earth, we beseech Thee to have mercy upon us as a people in this time of financial distress and difficulty. We humble ourselves before Thee, and confess that we have often cared too much for mere earthly prosperity, and have not sought as our first object Thy Kingdom and Thy righteousness. From all covetous and selfish desires, and from inordinate love of riches, deliver us, we pray Thee; increase in our land that righteousness which exalteth a nation; and remove, by the inworking of Thy Holy Spirit, all that now hinders the spread of godliness, equity, and concord among us. Grant this, we beseech Thee, for the glory of Thy holy name, through Jesus Christ our Saviour. Amen."

With the first sentence omitted, this prayer would read like an invocation to heaven to punish the Australians for their avarice, their selfishness, and their greed of money, by sending a financial crisis. As it stands, the only way in which I can read it is as follows :

"Almighty God, whose divine providence ordereth the rise and fall of the markets, we humbly approach Thy throne to promise Thee that if Thou wilt reëstablish confidence, cause the banks to reopen their doors, and the shareholders to receive good dividends, we will try to cure ourselves of avarice, selfishness, and greed of money."

What an easy, comfortable religion is that of certain Anglo-Saxons, who, satisfied that the Divinity has nothing to do but look after His peculiar people, are forever putting up petitions in which are set forth all their little wishes and wants.

CHAPTER XIX.

The Australian Newpapers—The Large Dailies—Weekly Editions—*The Australasian*—The Comic Papers—The Society Papers—The *Bulletin*.

OF all the achievements which Australia can justly boast of, there is not one which surpasses what she has accomplished in the way of journalism.

I do not know, in Europe or in America, any papers which have more serious value than many which are published daily in Victoria and New South Wales: the *Argus* and the *Age* in Melbourne, the *Morning Herald* and the *Daily Telegraph* in Sydney. These papers, composed of eight, and sometimes ten, large pages, are sold at a penny, and are from every point of view as well edited and as well informed as the *Daily News*, *Daily Telegraph*, the *Standard* and the *Daily Chronicle* of London. They have not perhaps the literary value of the *Journal des Débâts* or of the Paris *Figaro*, but they are much more complete in the matter of news. They strike a happy medium between the English daily papers and the American ones, being less sensational in style than the latter, but decidely brighter in tone than the former.

One wonders with amazement how a country so young can keep alive, and even richly flourishing, such daily papers as these, besides numerous and excellent evening papers, such as the *Evening News*, the *Echo*, and the *Star*, in Sydney; the *Standard* and the *Herald* in Melbourne. The *Melbourne Age* was printing a hundred thousand copies a day when I was in Australia; and when one of the partners withdrew, the sum that had to be paid to him was a hundred and fifty thousand pounds sterling. It is really impossible to overpraise the spirit of activity that has rendered such papers an absolute necessity.

Adelaide and Brisbane also have very good newspapers— the *Register* and the *Advertiser* in the first-named city, the *Courier* and the *Telegraph* in the second.

In New Zealand, too, you find first-class papers; at the head of the list are the *Auckland Herald*, the *Times*, the *Post*, and the *Press*, of Wellington; the *Times* and the *Press* of Christchurch, and the *Otago Times* of Dunedin.

Most of these papers publish a special weekly edition, which attains colossal proportions. Among these the palm must be given to the *Australasian*, published every Saturday by the *Melbourne Argus* Company. In the editing, the importance, the interest, and quantity of the matter printed, it is a journalistic *tour de force*, and nothing less. The *Town and Country Journal*, the *Mail*, the *Leader*, are also most remarkable weekly publications.

Scientific and literary papers, comic papers, among which must be mentioned the *Melbourne Punch*, religious papers, and agricultural journals—all interests are represented.

For local news, every suburb, every little town, has its newspaper. I have seen them in little towns of a few hundred inhabitants; every man makes it his duty to buy them, and, better still, there are some who make it a duty to read them.

I pass over a number of so-called Society papers, which interest me but little. However, mention must be made of the *Bulletin* of Sydney. In its way, it is the most scathing, most daring, the wittiest, the most impudent and best edited paper I know. Nothing quite so audacious exists, even in America, where all sorts of journalistic audacities are permitted.

The tone affected by this paper is national, that is, anti-English. Its motto is, "Australia for the Australians." All the political, social, and religious marionettes are treated with a cool impudence that is unmatchable.

The *Bulletin* is devoured by the masses, who delight in its democratic tone, and by Society, with a capital *S*, which finds in it the minutest details of the toilettes worn at a Government House ball, or at Mrs. So-and-So's garden party, as well as the most appetizing bits of gossip of the week served up with *sauce piquante*.

The circulation of this paper is enormous. You meet with it everywhere: it is on the tables of all the clubs and hotels, not of New South Wales alone, but of all the Colonies, including New Zealand and Tasmania; and if you go into the Bushman's hut, there are a hundred chances to one that you will find the latest number there.

This paper exposes many follies, many impostures; and the scourging it administers, without respect of persons, to snobs, humbugs, hypocrites, renders a service to Australian society. But that which counter-balances the good it does, and tends to make the publication a harmful one, is its alimentation of that very characteristic Australian trait—want of respect for what is respectable, and its encouragement of affectation in a certain section of Australians, by lending its columns to the chronicling of all their little sayings and doings.

The *Bulletin* is constantly guilty of the very failings that it so cleverly satirizes in the public who read it.

CHAPTER XX.

Amusements at the Antipodes—The Australian Gayer than the Englishman—Melbourne—Lord Hopetoun—The Racing Craze—The Melbourne Cup—Flemington Compared with Longchamps and Epsom.

THE Australian is still much too young to have strongly marked characteristic traits; but of all the members of the great Anglo-Saxon family, I think he is destined to become the most easy-going, the most sociable, and perhaps the most cheerful.

He is not, like the eastern American, the descendant of a sad, austere race. His ancestors were adventurers, and not fanatic Puritans, enemies of joy and happiness, seeking a corner of the world where they might freely give themselves up to their gloomy religion.

You will not find in the Australian that dogged, obstinate perseverance, that bull-dog tenacity which has helped the English to do so many great things, and which still puts the Scotchman beyond competition in every enterprise which calls for privations, hard work, and indomitable tenacity.

For the Australian, life has always been relatively easy. He had no formidable savage race to combat nor wild beasts to exterminate. Rigorous winters he knows nothing of. A sun, that lights and warms him. shines all the year round from an almost cloudless sky.

Even the vagrant, who lives on the generosity of the squatter at whose door he knocks at sunset, needs no other roof than a blanket, which, with his "billy," forms all his equipment. He lives in the open air. Even if brighter days should never dawn for him, he has enough to eat, pure air to breathe, he suffers neither from hunger nor cold, he is free, he has the sun to cheer him by day, and myriads of stars make his night beautiful. He can almost enjoy his life, which is incontestably pleasanter than that of the miner or the worker in a manufactory. In Australia, there is no real poverty except in Melbourne and Sydney. And even there, I do not know of any employment which would not allow a man, with a few months of thrift, to save enough to start a little farm in the Bush, if he were ready to be his own laborer.

The Australian has quite a passion for amusement. There is no country in the world whose people flock in such numbers to theatres, concerts, exhibitions, all places of recreation; there are no people who take so many holidays or enter with such keenness into all national sports; there is no society that dines and dances quite so much as Australasian society.

The pleasures of the lower classes are loud, and often vulgar; but the Australian gives himself up to them with more gaiety than the Englishman. Look at John Bull when he plays a game of foot-ball, or stands up in a sparring-match. He puts on a frowning, almost ferocious, face, that would make you believe that it is the honor of his country he is defending against some enemy who has sworn its destruction.

An English ballroom of the present day is not always a scene of great gaiety; there is a half-bored look on too many of the faces, and a lack of spontaneity about the enjoyment of the dancing. At the Government House balls in Sydney and Melbourne, I was struck with the look of pleasure on all the faces; it was not a duty—a function, as the English call it—that people were going through with. The dancing was full of spirit, and the dancers were really enjoying themselves; the whole scene was exhilarating.

And how could one help being gay at the Melbourne Government House, when the host was the young Earl of Hopetoun? This young diplomatist is about thirty years old, has a face that is bright and smiling, an intelligent forehead, and a delicate nose and mouth. He is witty and amiable, full of life, *Grand Seigneur* to the tips of his fingers, immensely rich, and generous in proportion. Not only all his salary goes in hospitality and acts of generosity, but he spends his large income besides. When he has been Governor five years, and quits Melbourne for Europe, the Victorians had better put on mourning; they will never again have Lord Hopetoun's equal.

But of all the amusements to which the Australians give themselves up, there is nothing that touches horse-racing for popularity. It is a dominant passion—a craze.

The combative instinct of the Anglo-Saxon, the love of competition, of struggle, of chance, of adventures, of facile gains, the passion for the horse, which in Australia is man's companion from his tenderest childhood, —all these things explain the fever that seizes on the Australian, when a few horses, mounted by jockeys in multi-colored attire, are on the course quivering with impatience for the signal to start,

I think nothing must astonish the visitor to Australia more than to see the tremendous hold horse-racing has taken upon the whole population. During Cup Week in Melbourne, scarcely anything but racing is thought of or talked of. Every train that comes into the city for a week beforehand brings crowds of people from all parts of Australasia. In Europe, certain sets of people go to races; in Australia, the whole population. Men, women, and children, of the best colonial society, have made bets on the horses; business men, clerks, servants, the very vagrants, all are interested in the result. There is not a little corner in any part of the Australian Bush where the conversation does not turn on the result of the race.

The greatest event of the year, in colonial life, is the Melbourne Cup Race. The prize is worth ten thousand pounds sterling; and such is the betting done upon this race, that when the winning horse is announced, more than five hundred thousand pounds change hands.

The banks are closed, trade is suspended, and the whole colony is breathless with feverish impatience, until the name of the winner of the Cup is published throughout the length and breadth of the land. It is a national event, only to be compared, for widespread intensity, to the presidential election in America—with this difference, that the Americans bet still more heavily on the event.

I went to see the Cup Race. It was frightful weather, but in spite of the pouring rain, there were nearly a hundred thousand people on the grounds, that is to say, one-tenth of the entire population of the colony. Had the weather been fine, the crowd would have been much larger still. In such weather, the Parisians would have hesitated at the idea of going to Auteuil or Longchamps, but here were people who had come a five days' sea voyage from New Zealand, others who had taken long journeys over land, others who had come from Tasmania, to see the racing; and what was the rain to them?

There were the Governors of three colonies, accompanied by their ladies and suites; there were members of the Legislative Council, who, having just passed a severe Bill against betting, had adjourned for Cup Week; there was the pick of Australian society, with its brave array of lovely women in elegant attire.

"Some important affair of State," said I to a friend, "is, I suppose, the cause of this rendez-vous between the Governors?"

"Certainly," he replied; "the Cup Race is the most important event of the year."

The racing takes place at Flemington, a village a few miles out of Melbourne. The race-course is vast, and all the arrangements perfect. Spacious stands, luxurious rooms of all sorts, lunch-rooms, tea-rooms, to suit all tastes and all purses, retiring rooms, toilet-rooms, refreshment bars, cigar divans, etc., where all articles offered for sale have been duly examined by the committee. Well might Lord Rosebery exclaim, when we went to see a race at Flemington, "This is not a race-meeting, it is more like a drawing-room entertainment." I should rather call it a garden party, with some first-class racing thrown in; a gigantic national picnic, at which the organizers have forgotten nothing that can conduce to the enjoyment of the party. No riotous behavior mars the scene, which, even on the flat where the masses congregate, is singularly free from coarseness and drunkenness.

I could not help comparing Flemington with the two great national race-courses of Europe, Epsom and Longchamps; and, as far as the arrangements for the comfort and enjoyment of the people are concerned, Flemington certainly stands first.

As a spectacle and as a holiday, the *Grand Prix* at Longchamps carries off the palm. It is an unique sight. The crowd of elegantly dressed people in the endless stream of carriages, unmarred by a shabby turn-out, much less a costermonger's cart, the thousands of the working classes massed on the green slopes overlooking the course, the merry picnickings in the woods around, make up a scene that pleases the eye and gladdens the heart. A week's work has not been sacrificed over the merrymaking, nor a week's earnings gone in bets and carousings; the outing does not result in a crop of police court cases, but a day's rational pleasure is taken, and refreshes for to-morrow's work.

But if Flemington cannot show such a refined crowd as Longchamps, it exhibits none of the revolting rowdyism of Epsom.

It is strange that in England, the very nursery of racing and of its *raison d'être*, the blood horse, the sight of that great English race, the Derby, should be spoilt by the disorderliness of the crowd. It is stranger still that, in England, the home of propriety, you should have to confront repulsive sights, which might easily be suppressed, if only a little decent thoughtfulness were exercised in providing for the needs of such a mass of people out for the day so far from town; not that even an angel from heaven could make an orderly crowd out of the terribly mixed material that flows into Epsom on Derby Day.

At Flemington, you have a respectable crowd, composed for the most part of people who have come there in the hope of winning a little money. At Epsom, you have the British contrast of the unbridled luxury of the rich, and the vulgar revelry of the lower classes. At Longchamps, you have a rendezvous for high society, a family *fête* for the middle classes, and a day of healthy recreation for the people.

CHAPTER XXI.

The Drama in the Colonies—Madame Sarah Bernhardt in Australia—Anglo-Saxon Theatres Compared with Theatres in Paris—Variety Shows—The Purveyor of Intellectual Pleasures—An Important Actor—The Theatre in Small Towns.

THE Australians are great lovers of the theatre. English companies, composed of from sixty to eighty performers, do not fear to go to the enormous expense of the voyage. They carry their costumes and scenery, and, after a six months' Australasian tour, generally return much enriched.

Madame Bernhardt herself had no cause to regret her visit to the Colonies. In Sydney, Melbourne, and Adelaide, three years since, she reaped an ample harvest of guineas and applause. I should not like to affirm that all the spectators knew enough of French to appreciate the delicacy, finish and power of the great *tragédienne;* but they went in crowds to see her, and thus thank her in person for having been good enough to consider the Colonies as a field of operation worth exploiting by the greatest actress of modern times.

Melbourne and Sydney possess handsome theatres, quite as well appointed as those of England and America, and the comfort of the audience is much more studied in them than it is in the Parisian theatres. When you have paid for your ticket, you are at the end of your trouble, and you have nothing to do but take your pleasure. In Paris, when you have taken your ticket, which is not numbered, your troubles begin, and this ticket only serves to bandy you from one tyrant to another: from the gentleman in swallow-tail and white cravat, with a salary of four francs fifty, who treats you with high and mighty indifference, to the bearded harpy who packs you away just where she likes unless you grease her paw with silver, and who worries you with a little footstool which you have no earthly need of, until you long to tell her to go, she and her wooden stool, to swell Satan's bonfire, and rid you of her purrings and whinings. Is there in this world a public more easily tyrannized over than that good, easy-going Parisian one? Is there a city more bound down by routine? Is it, after all, so impossible to have, in Parisian theatres, as in English and American ones, numbered tickets, that allow the theatre-goer to proceed in peace to the stall bearing the number of the ticket he has purchased, without being obliged to plead and tip attendants to obtain the seat that belongs to him?

In the theatres of all Anglo-Saxon countries—that is to say, free countries, where common sense reigns and the public is master—when you have bought your theatre ticket, it gives you the right to a numbered seat, to a programme, which is as indispensable at the play as is the bill of fare at a restaurant, and to a peg in the cloakroom upon which to hang an overcoat, without having to submit to the annoyance of a crowd of abject mendicants, who have no reason to be in the theatre except as obliging servants of the public.

The theatres I was speaking of do still better than this. They are all provided with bars, smoke-rooms, lavatories, ladies' cloakrooms—in a word, every convenience which the managers think it their duty to place at the disposal of the public which brings them its money.

If the Australian theatres are comfortable, the intellectual entertainments served up are mostly wretched productions.

I saw a few excellent actors who have become, so to speak, Australian : Messrs. Brough and Boucicault (the latter is a son of the celebrated actor), Mr. Tetharidge in comedy, and Mr. Walter Bentley in drama and tragedy; but the pieces that have the greatest success with the mass of the public are cock-and-bull affairs which the Montmartre Theatre would reject with disdain, a succession of songs and dances in costume, commonly called Variety Shows—a Folies-Bergère programme of the most vulgar and stupid description. There comes on the stage a man with a red nose, a bald cranium six inches high, surmounted by a hat too ridiculously small to stay on his head. He pretends to be helplessly drunk. He sings, dances, and falls on the stage; gets up, sings and dances again, and again falls down. And this amuses the people for a quarter of an hour. Then there will appear a dozen girls, generally pretty and always lightly dressed. They dance, singing the while; and they in their turn give place to some other mountebank, who will also dance. An Australian who cannot dance a jig would be a useless piece of furniture in the theatre.

For her intellectual entertainments, Australia depends

upon Messrs. R. S. Smythe & Son, who have never disappointed her. These celebrated impresarios give the Australians an opportunity of hearing the greatest artistes and the best-known European lecturers. Under their direction have appeared Madame Arabella Goddard, Mr. Charles Santley, Sir Charles and Lady Hallé, Mr. Archibald Forbes, whose lectures on his experiences as a war correspondent had attracted all England, Mr. G. A. Sala, Mr. H. M. Stanley, and numerous others.

Nothing is more amusing in the Colonies than to listen to the speeches that the public force the principal actor to make when the play is over. (In America I have even seen an audience insist on a speech between each act. When the last act but one was finished, the actor excused himself on the ground of having to don for the last act a costume which it took him ten minutes to put on.)

Those speeches are generally composed of flattery addressed to the spectators. The actor comes forward, thanks the public for having honored him with its confidence, and promises in the future to continue to use all his efforts to merit the appreciation that it has accorded to him in the past. Then he speaks of his art, his receipts, and his private affairs.

I one day heard, in Melbourne, an actor, who has made himself a reputation by his singing of comic songs and his dancing of jigs, make the following remarks in public: " Ladies and gentlemen, I have read in the papers of this city that Dan G. (the name of a *confrère*) and I had fallen out. I wish to give a formal denial to this statement. Dan and I have always been the best of friends. We are both successful enough not to be jealous of each other, and I beg you to believe that our relations are of the most cordial kind."

And the public applauded.

Bismarck in Parliament, refuting the statement that he and the Emperor of Germany had quarreled, could not have made his statement with more seriousness. It was highly comical.

But you should see the melodramas that are played in the smaller towns; you could but admire the endurance of the public which swallows such stuff, and you could but pity the fate of those poor strolling players, knocking about from town to town, thankful when the receipts will allow them to pay their hotel bill and buy their railway tickets to their next destination.

These plays are a succession of fifteen or twenty scenes, in each of which the heroine is on the point of succumbing to the infernal machinations of the traditional stage villain, when the hero, who happens to be at hand, rushes to her rescue. The curtain falls, and the worthy folk in the auditorium breathe freely again. The curtain rises once more. The villain has succeeded in seducing the young girl. He announces to her his intention of abandoning her.

"But I love you," cries the unhappy one.

"What is that to me?" replies the villain; "do you think I will have anything more to do with such a degraded creature as you? Begone, or I shall kill you."

But it happens that the hero is not far off. He seizes the villain, who, to keep his hand in, has killed the girl's father. The poor father had done him no harm, but when one is a villain in melodrama one has a reputation to keep up. The hero then seizes the wretch, passes a rope around his arms, and ties him to a chair. The villain might go off, taking the chair with him, but he accepts his position as inevitable. He does not stir, but awaits his fate. He does not wait in vain. Scarcely has the hero gone for the police, when a friend of the villain, who happens to be there, cuts his cords and sets him at liberty; but just as he is escaping, a friend of the young girl, who happens to be near, seizes the wretch, casts the cords around his arms, and binds him to the chair once more. He is very strong, this friend of the girl, so the villain and his accomplice content themselves with looking at him, without stirring a muscle, while he goes through the business.

In the next act, the unhappy girl is wandering the country in search of a refuge. She falls fainting by the wayside. The villain appears on the scene, and roughly rouses her.

" For ever in my path," says he; "better make an end of this."

" Do not kill me," she cries.

Happily, a friend who happens to be passing that way—

At the end of the twentieth scene the villain is caught. No one happens to be there to deliver him, and the play is ended.

This tricky trash is made up by the actor-manager of the company, is advertised as " immensely successful in the Colonies," and is often signed with the most celebrated names of the day, especially those which happen to be on the public tongue at the moment.

Thus the production that I have just described was signed "C. H. Spurgeon." It was just at the time when the great preacher and philanthropist had died, and his name was on every one's lips.

When Mr. H. M. Stanley had returned to Europe after having finished a brilliant lecturing tour in Australia, the plays of this kind were signed " Stanley " for several months.

CHAPTER XXII.

Railroads in the Colonies—You Set Out but You Do Not Arrive—A Woman in a Hurry—Mixed Trains—First-Class Travelers—Curious Traveling Companions.

"In these days," has remarked a French writer, whose name I cannot remember, "people no longer travel—they set out and they arrive."

In the Colonies, you set out, but you do not arrive.

With the exception of the express trains between Sydney, Melbourne, and Adelaide, the speed is seldom more than ten miles an hour. They are indeed ordinary trains, and every time I traveled in one I thought that there was no safer place in this world than one of these colonial trains. You are sure to arrive safe and sound, but if you are in a hurry, a buggy is better. In France, we have the same word for funeral procession and ordinary trains, *convoi*. It is not so in Australia, but there is so much resemblance in the things, if not the names, that when we passed one of those trains I instinctively lifted my hat.

It is with the greatest difficulty in the world that the engine-driver succeeds in not arriving before the time stated on the railway time-tables. He does his best: stops at stations where no one wants to get in or out; draws up at every shed on the line, in the hope of some one wanting to entrust him with a letter or a parcel; if he sees a few boys playing foot-ball or cricket in a field, I verily believe he stops his train to look at them. In spite of all this, it is as much as he can do not to arrive before his time. I have seen people stop the train as you stop an omnibus in the street.

The colonials themselves take the thing in good part, and are full of amusing stories on the subject.

Here is one among a hundred :

The engine-driver of a train sees a poor old woman tramping along the road with a wearied step. Struck with compassion for her, he stops his train, invites her to get in, and says he will take her as far as the next station.

" Many thanks ; I should be very glad to accept, but I am in a hurry," she replies.

The state of things is easily explained, however.

In the Colonies, the railways are made by the Government and belong to the State. For reasons of economy, a narrow gauge was adopted, and it would be dangerous for running rapid trains upon. By going at slow speed, coal is economized, and as, outside the great towns, the population is not important enough to pay for the luxury of express trains, the Government is obliged to have omnibus trains, which, once a day only, stop at all stations, and, if necessary, in certain unpeopled localities, where sheds have been put up so as to allow some squatter of the neighborhood to join or leave the train, by making a sign to the driver to stop the train there.

Besides this slow train there is a goods train, to which there is a carriage attached for the convenience of such persons as may not have a horse available and are too lazy to walk. This kind is called a mixed train in the Colonies. You find it also in the United States.

The Americans, who are nothing if not humorous, have given it the name of *accommodation train*.

Give the Colonies time to develop themselves, and I guarantee that one of these days their trains will put those of the English South-Eastern line to shame. The express trains that form the communication between the capitals are already as rapid as the best European ones, and quite as comfortable.

In New Zealand and South Africa, the trains have third-class compartments for the use of the colored population. In Australia, the blacks do not count for anything, and society is divided into two classes, first and second. However, in a country where everyone is afraid of not impressing upon every one else the fact that he is as good as his neighbor, or better, I was not surprised to see the second-class carriages empty and the first-class all full, in spite of the stagnation of business and the fear of bankruptcy before the eyes of half the population.

In England, when you ask for a ticket for any station, you are handed a third-class one. In Australia, unless you mention second, you are handed a ticket for first class.

Many a time did I long to slip into a second-class carriage to avoid the crowd and stretch out at ease among the cushions. It was not to be thought of. If ever I had allowed myself such a luxury, and had been discovered in a second-class carriage, the thing would have been bruited about, and all my chances of success shattered. The Australians are not a careful people exactly, but they are very careful of appearances.

What queer traveling companions you may have to put up with!

First, there is the bore, who arouses you from a sweet, refreshing sleep to give you the name of the squatter who owns the lands you are passing through, explains how the father came to settle there, tells you the fortune he made there, and relates in detail the history of the family.

The one I most dreaded was the man who recognized me, and, having heard one or several of my lectures, went through them again, interlarding them with commentaries, and explaining to me the points.

One, a little bolder than the rest, but whose frankness I could but admire, picked them to pieces.

Several times did obliging stationmasters reserve a compartment for our party. To such I owe an eternal debt of gratitude.

Very often those people had the very best intentions in the world, I am sure; but alas! hell is paved with them, and is probably none the more agreeable for that. I was once tapped on the shoulder. "Hallo, Max, where is your compartment?" said a worthy fellow, with a frank and honest face. "I am going to travel with you. Come and have a drink before starting!"

The good fellows offered me cigars, and did their best to make me understand that they were happy to be in my company. It would have been bad taste to be frigid with them. But I would fain have said to them, "A man who has been traveling incessantly during two years, who has to spend six, seven or eight hours a day in a train, and has to speak for two hours every night, appreciates as much quiet as he can get."

CHAPTER XXIII.

Spirit of Nationality and Independence—Local Patriotism—
Every Man for Himself and the Colonies for the Colonials.

OF all the English Colonies, I think that Canada is the most faithful to England. The proximity of the United States is the cause of this. If Canada were isolated, or situated at the antipodes, its spirit of national independence would be as strong as that of the young generation of Australia or South Africa. The fear of being swallowed up in the United States keeps the Canadians loyal to England. If they must belong to some one, they think that there is more prestige in belonging to England than to America. This, at any rate, is the feeling of the Canadian upper classes. Those who only think of the Treaty of Commerce with the United States, which imposes a duty of thirty per cent. upon all merchandise crossing the frontier on either side, those people would be in favor of annexation to-morrow. As to the masses, as I have said elsewhere, they are divided into four camps.

In Australia, national aspirations are very strong, especially among those who, born in the Colonies, have known no other country. To be sure, the Australians are as free as the English; they govern themselves as they think fit, and have no tribute to pay to England, who, on the contrary, confides to them much capital. Only the presence of the Governor in their midst reminds them that they are not a nation, but merely a dependency, and this irritates certain Anglo-Saxons, who, brought up in the nursery of liberty, do not understand why it is necessary to belong to anybody. The Governor governs much less than King Log; but there he is, and in the eyes of many Australians even this is too much. No one as yet thinks of demanding autonomy for the Australasian Colonies, but the idea is germinating in the brain. At present the Australians beg the mother-country to be so good as to consult them upon the choice of a Governor. Soon they will exact it. Next, they will make their own choice, and eventually they may dispense with him altogether.

In the South African Colonies, where the Dutch element is more or less hostile to England, this sentiment is much stronger still.

The love of liberty and independence is so deep-rooted in the Englishman, that when he has established himself in one of the Colonies, he can scarcely understand why his new country should not be perfectly free and independent. His patriotism becomes local, all his interest becomes centered in the new country, and, curiously enough, the next generations born in the Colonies have almost a feeling of dislike for England—the England which has founded their country, but which, by sending it a Governor, reminds them that they do not belong to a free nation. And the proof of this is, that the Australian or South African politician has not the least chance of success unless he poses before the electors as a patriot who will defend the interests of the Colonies against any encroachments attempted by the mother-country.

If the Colonies should one day decide to proclaim

their independence, England will be powerless to prevent it.

It will be her fault for giving them an excuse, but it will ever be to her glory to have given them the means.

In founding new worlds in distant oceans, and in teaching her children to go and build up free nations, England deserves well of humanity. It is far more glorious to have founded the United States than to have conquered India. The United States provide a home for seventy million human beings. India provides berths for a few thousand Englishmen.

If the Colonies should declare their independence, England's prestige would suffer, but the evil would go no further. John Bull is so little master in his Colonies, that his products are taxed there as if they were entering a foreign country. The service of the great steamship lines between London and Sydney, or London and the Cape, would not be interrupted. The only difference would probably be the increased number of passengers on board.

John Bull is so little master in his own outhouses, that when the Chartered Company the other day took the resolution of exterminating the Matabeles and taking possession of their country, a territory almost as large as France, the English were not even consulted.

"Stay where you are," said the Company to John Bull; "we are strong enough to do the business."

A few English protested, and the Government of Her Britannic Majesty ordered the High Commissioner for South Africa to demand explanations. Mr. Cecil Rhodes, Premier of the Colony, replied in the plainest terms, requesting that the English would mind their own business, saying that he would mind his, and that he had no account to render to any but the people of South Africa. The Governor pocketed the reply, transmitted it to John Bull, who, in turn, pocketed it, and consoled himself for the snub by ordering his mapmakers to mark in red Matabeleland, the new possession acquired by the firm, John Bull & Co.

John did still better.

The papers published the number of Matabeles *killed*, and the number of Anglo-African volunteers *massacred*, in the various engagements that were fought on Lobengula's territory. And that which gives added humor to the terms chosen is, that the soldiers of the Company *killed* the Matabeles with Maxim guns, while the poor savages had only staves and assegais wherewith to *massacre* the invaders of their native land.

If the poor Matabeles had been provided with Maxim guns and Martinis, Mr. Rhodes would have intimated to John Bull the necessity of sending out to Africa several regiments of red-coats; but as this was not the case, Mr. Rhodes and the people whom he governs by the grace of God and the good pleasure of Mr. Hofmeyr, can boast that the glory of having exterminated the Matabeles belongs to them entirely.

CHAPTER XXIV.

Tasmania—The Country—The Inhabitants of Other Days and the Inhabitants of the Present Day—Visit to the Depots—Survivors of the " Ancien Régime "—A Tough old Scotchwoman—A Touching Scene—Launceston and Hobart.

TASMANIA has quite a European look. It is like a bit of Normandy or Devonshire, with its woods and hills, its flowers, its hedges of wild rose and hawthorn. Nothing is grandiose, but all is pretty and picturesque. It is an English landscape in the most perfect climate imaginable.

But how is it possible that a land so privileged by nature comes to be inhabited by such an uninteresting population? I never saw any people more peaceful, more ordinary, more bourgeois, more provincial, more behind the times. It is the kind of people one meets in little country towns in England on Sundays after church. You may still see commonly in Tasmania the old-fashioned Englishwoman with long curls and a mushroom hat, the classic Englishwoman, such as George Cruikshank drew for the pages of Charles Dickens' novels. She is just as narrow and thin as he drew her, with a lenten face, and looking as if she lived on tea and toast. Happily, there are also plenty of pretty women to be seen, who are remarkable for their freshness and beauty.

Is it possible that this country, now so tranquil and in the full enjoyment of peace and plenty, can once have resounded to the sound of clanking fetters, imprecations, and cries of suffering humanity ? Can it be here that such scenes were enacted as Marcus Clarke described in his famous book, *For the Term of his Natural Life!*

Tasmania was once a penal settlement, beside which our New Caledonia of to-day is a very Garden of Eden. There, English convicts were chastised with chastisements worthy of the Middle Ages or of the Inquisition. The slightest infraction of discipline was punished with the lash on the naked back of the unhappy wretch who had offended. The lash was the cat-o'-nine-tails, and the punishment often went so far as a hundred strokes. But all the horrors, are they not written in the book of Marcus Clarke! At Port Arthur is still to be seen the place where these legal atrocities took place, in the presence of clergy, and sanctioned by a House of Lords containing two archbishops and twenty-four bishops, who never lifted their voices against such infamy.

The first shipload of convicts reached Tasmania from England in 1817, the last in 1853. In all, 66,243 convicts were sent to this penal station between these two dates.

A curious fact. Of all the countries of the world, Tasmania is the one where, in proportion to its population, the fewest crimes are committed.

Tasmania has some old convicts whom she keeps in depôts, where life is made as easy as may be for them. The director, who showed me over one of these buildings, is full of untiring kindness to the poor creatures. Former sufferings have made lunatics of many, and maimed many others. A few of the figures were bent double. Not one face that I saw betrayed a spirit of vengeance or hatred; I even failed to discover a sign of anguish or misery. The eyes were haggard, and their light gone out; they betrayed no sentiment but resignation and indifference. The inmates have full freedom in the depôt, wander freely in their gardens, which are public, and go into the town when they please. They are well fed, well clothed, and well cared for. The townspeople frequent their gardens, and the children play around them. They even have a theatre, where kind-hearted folk give them occasional treats in the way of a concert or a comedy.

These poor wretches, whom I had talks with, seem to have forgotten for the most part where they came from, or to whom they belonged. They are no longer of this world. There are many of them who do not even remember what they did to merit transportation. It is complete oblivion of life, a dazed numbness created by great sufferings. There was one among others, known by the name of Bill, who had been at Launceston forty-seven years. He is an idiot, and passes the days in laughter. Ask him what brought him to Tasmania, and he will reply, still laughing, "Handkerchief, sir." "Stolen?" "Yes, sir." "Where?" "Bethnal Green" Do not ask him anything else. Handkerchief—stolen—Bethnal Green, such is the sum of his vocabulary. The voyage out, the arrival in Tasmania, the labor, the punishments, the fifty-six pound fetters that were fastened to his ankles, the lash—he remembers nothing, not even his parents. Handkerchief—stolen—Bethnal Green; when he is not saying these three words, he is laughing.

I went to the depôt provided with some tobacco for the men and bon-bons for the women.

I had divided the tobacco into eighty packets of an ounce each. I distributed these little gifts with some small money to these poor wretches as I met with them in the buildings and the gardens. On a bench two men were seated. I sat down beside them, and offered to the one nearest me his share. "Thank you, sir," he said to me; "but you do not recognize me. You have already given me some tobacco and money; will you give it to Jack, here? he has not had any."

In what strange places honesty will hide! thought I. This poor fellow had not at all a bad face, but just looked stupid and resigned. I asked him what crime he had committed to be where he was. He did not know in the least. The director himself could not enlighten me on the point.

The thing that struck me most on observing the faces around was the absence of intelligence. Few of the countenances were evil-looking, but all were stamped with stupidity. And I thought of the saying of our great jurisconsult, "It is only the fools who are in the prisons; the cleverest malefactors are at large."

I left the men's quarters to go and visit the women. What a hideous sight! Veritable old hags, worthy to figure in *Macbeth*, with toothless mouths, puffy, colorless faces, and tufted chins. A perfect nightmare. I gave them their sweets; most of them asked me for tobacco. They accepted the sugar stuff, but with scanty thanks.

"The women give me far more trouble than the men," said the director. "They are less resigned, they are always grumbling, and when they go into the town they get drunk with the money that is given to them by the townspeople."

There was one old soul who struck the comic note amid this chorus of grumblings and discontent. She was a Scotchwoman, to whom the magistrate had just given six months' imprisonment, which meant that for six months to come she would not be able to go in the town and get drunk. "Yes, sir, sax months for a wee drap o' drrrink, the blackguard!" This, it seems, was one whom nothing can subjugate. When the six months are over, she is sure to roll into the gutter again. Meanwhile she utters harangues full of threats.

A touching scene. In the yard was a young mother undergoing a month's imprisonment. Her children were there with her, and ladies from the town had brought toys and sweets for the little creatures, who, ignorant of their surroundings, looked radiant with health and happiness.

A curious detail. The director, pointing out to me one of the women, tells me that she and her husband have been forty years in Tasmania, and have met several times without recognizing each other.

I am willing to believe this; but, looking at the woman, a horrible harpy, with a snarling and repulsive-looking face, I think the husband must thank his stars that here, as well as in public baths, there is men's side and women's side. Recognize his wife! Not he!

Tasmania has but two towns of any importance, Launceston, and Hobart, the capital. The first of these has nothing remarkable about it but a superb gorge situated at the entrance to the town, and a post office, the grotesque architecture of which, half Flemish, half Moorish, as it is, ought to be sufficient to keep the inhabitants in a constant state of hilarity. The gorge, along the bottom of which a rapid torrent rushes between two most picturesque wooded hills, is inducement enough for any traveler to alight at Launceston.

ENTRANCE TO THE GORGE, LAUNCESTON.

Hobart is incontestably one of the loveliest spots I have visited.

After flat, brown, dusty, hurrying Melbourne, it was delicious to ramble about this, old-fashioned town and its lovely hills. The tram-car bell had not yet tolled the knell of old-fashioned peace and graceful repose, but the rails were laid, and cars to run on them were being landed.

Hobart is charming, whether you sit on the shore and look on the blue waters of the harbor, hedged about everywhere by ranges of grand hills, the foremost green with an almost English verdure, the more distant ones blue with a blueness very un-English; or whether you

HOBART, LOOKING FROM MOUNT WELLINGTON.

wander up through the straggling town to make nearer acquaintance with the great hills that tower up behind it, getting a thrill of pleasure as Mount Wellington's grandeur gradually dawns on your senses. The splendid roads, all the work of the convicts of former days, making walking a pleasure. The one which winds up by the side of Mount Wellington, and leads to the

Huon river, is delightful. When you are a couple of miles out of Hobart, on this road, you have a charming view of the quaint jumble of houses that forms the little town, the clear, smooth water of the harbor it sits looking at, and the sweet, waving blue hills beyond. Here, too, you get a better idea of Mount Wellington's four thousand feet of grandeur than when you saw the giant from the town, not but what there are days when it seems to hang over the streets, almost menacing in its magnificence. The air is perfumed with the odor of sweet-briar. Hedges of this plant, covered with roses of the brightest pink, delighted our European eyes; but I am told that the Tasmanian farmer looks upon this thing of beauty as anything but a joy, and is forever doing battle with its bold tenacity of life.

Ascending all the time, and leaving Mount Wellington behind, you by and by get glimpses of the ocean on the left, away out between the hills; and the road winds along, under enormous tall trees, past deep gullies full of ferns and luxuriant flowering shrubs, past gigantic hawthorns that made one wish it was their flower-time instead of their seed-time. At every turn the scene changes. At one moment you are in a wood, and at the next there flashes upon you a sight of distant sea, and all the lovely country between you and it.

Speaking of flowering shrubs reminds me that even in Australia proper the wealth of wild flowers is remarkable. In that land of the one tree, there is an endless variety of wild flowers. Nature has been as lavish on the one hand as she has been niggardly on the other.

With all its "Sleepy Hollow" appearance, Hobart takes the lead of the cities on the mainland in some things. It was the first to open the doors of its interesting museum and picture gallery to the public on Sundays.

I would fain have spent a month wandering around Hobart.

Sir Robert Hamilton had just retired from the Governorship of Tasmania, and he and his charming wife were on their way to Europe when I reached Hobart. I regretted this all the more, in that, having had the pleasure of meeting Lady Hamilton in England and in Ireland, I should have been happy to spend a few moments in the company of this amiable and talented lady.

CHAPTER XXV.

New Zealand—Norway and Switzerland at the Antipodes—The Point of the Earth's Surface that is Farthest from Paris—The Towns—No Snakes, but a Great Many Scots—The Small Towns—A Curious Inscription.

OF all the English Colonies, New Zealand is one of the most prosperous and by a great deal the most picturesque.

The scenery is superb, a happy combination of all that Norway and Switzerland have to show in the way of gorges, lakes, and mountains. Add to this a perfect climate, a fertile soil, a well-spread population, intelligent and industrious, the upper classes of which are amiable, hospitable, and highly cultivated; a native population, agreeable, intelligent, and artistic; and you will admit that here is a privileged country where people ought to be content with their lot.

For that matter they are. They certainly might be with less.

I had not long to wait for the picturesque in New Zealand, for before landing at the Bluff, the southern point of the island, the steamer, out of pure amiability, went out of its direct route to enter the two most beautiful sheets of water of the south coast, Milford Sound and George Sound.

The entrance to Milford Sound is just wide enough to give passage to the boat, which for nearly an hour follows a narrow channel between immense perpendicular mountains. At every turn the scene changes, as if by enchantment. Scarcely have you fixed your gaze on some barren, rugged cliffs, when you have before your eyes a towering mountain clothed with ferns as tall as palm-trees, and of a bright green. Soon the passage widens and becomes a succession of little lakes, around which nature surpasses herself in chains of mountains

MILFORD SOUND, NEW ZEALAND—THE MITRE PEAK.

capped with eternal snow, gorges, cascades; and the Bush, such as one only sees it in New Zealand, of a radiant green freshness, an apparently impenetrable mass of ferns and lovely plants.

I had never seen anything so wild and picturesque, so entirely grandiose. I would have liked to be alone for an hour with this unique scenery.

George Sound, a few miles farther south, is almost as beautiful as Milford Sound.

I was interested to hear that if one could draw a line through the centre of the earth to the surface of the globe on the other side, it would come out a few leagues from Paris. Thus it is impossible, while on earth, for a Parisian to be farther from his beloved city than in George Sound.

DUNEDIN.

New Zealand possesses four important towns of from thirty-five to sixty thousand inhabitants—Dunedin, Christchurch, Wellington, and Auckland. It will not be long before the energetic population of Invercargill attains one of these figures.

The lucky inhabitants of this beautiful country have every blessing that can help them towards success—a perfect climate, a fertile soil, no wild animals, no snakes, and plenty of Scots.

Dunedin, capital of the province of Otago, is as Scotch as Edinburgh,* and more Scotch than Glasgow; so Scotch that the Chinese in Dunedin, in order to have any chance of earning their livelihood, are obliged to call themselves, not Lee-Wang or Chee-Wang, but MacWang.

CHRISTCHURCH.

Christchurch, on the contrary, is an extremely English town, an Anglican foundation with a choice society. It is not, like Dunedin, a centre of commercial activity: it is the rendezvous of colonial aristocracy, the Mayfair of the Colonies.

Wellington, at the south of the North Island, is the seat of government. The town is admirably situated, and has a picturesque harbor that brings back memories

* Edinburgh formerly was called Dunedin.

of Hobart, Tasmania. The largest wooden construction in the world is the Parliament House at Wellington. Its enormous dimensions do not detract from its grace. I found Wellington society delightful, most refined and charming; and here, as in the great Australian towns, the doors of good society hospitably open.

Auckland, a town of more than sixty thousand inhabitants, overlooking a beautiful harbor, is built on

WELLINGTON.

picturesque hills, from whence most beautiful views may be obtained. It is destined, by its exceptional situation and the energy of its inhabitants, to attain the importance of a Melbourne or a Sydney.

The rapidity with which these towns grow is prodigious. A commercial enterprise is launched. After a few weeks a public-house is built, a bank opens its doors, a newspaper is started, and population flows in and groups itself around this nucleus. In a very few years it has become a flourishing town. Not a soldier, not a functionary. This is what strikes a Frenchman, whose country is crippled by bureaucracy, bound down with red tape.

A witty French traveler, M. Georges Kohn, in his *Voyage autour Du Monde*, a volume full of clever observations and unflagging sprightliness, exclaims:

"In our Colonies, the first building is a police station; the second, that of the tax-collector; the third, a statistic office, and you have to wait for the colonists, who are to be looked after, taxed, judged, and especially counted by the census-taker."

AUCKLAND HARBOR, FROM CEMETERY GULLY.

In the English Colonies, the population first, the intervention of government afterwards. With us it is the government first, the population—where is it? It stays at home in France; and when our soldiers have guaranteed the tranquillity and security of a country, the English, the Germans, the Danes, the Swedes, the

Chinese, etc., etc., take up their abode there ; and the good French taxpayer at home asks, as he pays the bill, " *Ce qu'on est allé faire dans cette galère.*"

I warrant that, out of our thirty-six millions in France, there are not five hundred thousand who know just where the French Colonies are. I warrant that there is not in France a single mother (that woman whose empire is supreme at home) who does not oppose the emigration of her sons, and prefer for them situations as quill drivers at eighteen hundred francs a year. Try and found colonies while such sentiments reign ! The British Empire was founded by the spirit of independence instilled and alimented in the Englishman from his tenderest age, not only at school, but at home.

Besides the four great towns, mention must be made of Invercargill, Oamaru, Timaru, Nelson, Napier, Wanganui, Palmerston, all towns of from three to six thousand souls : Nelson, a gem, an idyll, a miniature Arcadia, a sleeping beauty ; Oamaru, with its street of palaces ; Wanganui, with a monument, the inscription upon which is a *chef-d'œuvre* of humor :

" To the memory of brave men who fell gloriously in the defence of law and order against barbarism and fanaticism."

You think, perhaps, that the brave men mentioned were the poor Maoris who were killed while defending their territory. Not at all ; they were the Englishmen who came to take possession of the country and deprive them of their liberty.

The towns of New Zealand are coquettishly built, the streets well kept, wide and straight. The large towns all possess excellent museums and fine public gardens.

The Australians, for whom a five days' sea voyage is a trifle, go in great numbers to New Zealand in the summer in order to escape the heat of their own country. If New Zealand were not more than five days' journey from Europe, our tourists would flock there every year also.

CHAPTER XXVI.

The Maoris—Types—Tattooing—Ways and Customs—Native Chivalry—The Legends of the Country—Sir George Grey—Lucky Landlords—The "Haka"—The Beautiful Victoria—Maori Villages—New Zealand the Prettiest Country in the World.

IN Maoriland you find a race of superb men coupled to hideous women. With the exception of the young girls, and here and there a woman of a Jewish or an Italian type, who are passable, among the Maoris the fair sex is the male sex.

The men are nearly all of the same type—tall, well-built, with a look of firmness and kindness in the eyes. It is easy to see you are in presence of a warlike but chivalrous race.

The women are of many types. I have seen, among the female Maoris, Jewesses, Spaniards, and Italians, negresses, and even the Australian type. The skin is of a deep bronze, the mouth enormous, the hair short, thick, and badly kept. The figure is of a heavy build, with large haunches and hanging breasts. When they are married, their lips and chin are tattooed.

Nothing is more comical than to see, in certain towns, these strange forms decked out in great loose gowns of white or pink, humped by tournures and crinolines (over and above those with which nature has amply provided them), and great felt hats stuck with feathers, and, to complete the picture, the mouth adorned with a short pipe, a regular navvy's comforter. These grotesque creatures have a coquetry of their own. Some

PAIKIA.
[*From a Photograph by* Foy Brothers, *Thames, New Zealand.*]

of them go so far as to have their backs tattooed, so as to be fascinating in the water when they swim; and I one day had as much as I could do to persuade a Maori belle that on this subject her word was quite sufficient for me.

With the men, tattooing has long been out of fashion, but among the older Maoris I saw marvelous examples of the practice. The forehead, nose, and cheeks are covered with a freehand design in dark blue, making the face repulsive but picturesque.

MAORI GREETING—RUBBING NOSES.
[*From a Photograph by* BURTON BROS., *Dunedin, New Zealand.*]

The Maori men are *Grands Seigneurs*, who make their women wait upon them, but who never ill-treat them. They adore children, and make excellent fathers.

When two Maoris meet, they are quietly demonstrative in their greetings. They press each other's hands, and remain, while one might count twenty, nose laid against nose, without movement, without speech—a few instants of mute exultation, of friendly ecstasy.

Their language is the softest in the world. Like those of the Samoans and Hawaiians, it contains, I am told, only thirteen letters. It is *K, P, L, N* that you seem to hear all the time. Here is some Maori; it is the notice posted in all the New Zealand railway stations: "*Kaua e Kai paipa Ki Konci*" (Smoking is Prohibited). It has very much the sound of Greek, has it not?

The volubility of the women is prodigious. It is a torrent, an avalanche of words. There are talkative women in all countries, but you would search the world in vain for a human being who could compete with a Maori woman. You should see these gossips sitting in the sun in a circle, pipe in mouth; above all, you should hear them! To get a faint idea of their chatter, picture to yourself a swarm of sparrows around a handful of crumbs. The conversation does not seem to consist of questions and answers, or of remarks suggested one by the other; all speak at once, without looking at one another, without appearing to listen one to the other, and loudly enough to make themselves giddy in a few moments. There is no pausing to take breath. While one cries at the top of her voice, "*Kolomo, Kalolulu, tarakiti, pikimolaka, rarapa;*" another vociferates, "*Kikiriki, ratatata, molakolululu;*" the others accompanying with, "*Karawera, Ratapuni, Kolololu, Molokulo;*" then all start together in chorus. It sets one's head whirling to listen to it. The faces of these women remain immobile, and have a slight smile. What a pity that jealousy should be unknown among them! a scene of jealousy, a war of words, between two of these chatterboxes would be something never to be forgotten. I have seen men try to take part in the conversation. They mildly ventured to give forth a "*Kolokulu*" or two, which no doubt signified, "Have you a moment to spare?" Then they sat down, and, having apparently given up all hope of getting a word in edgewise, listened calmly to the babble, or composed themselves to sleep.

The Maoris look on the married woman from the French rather than the English standpoint, when there has been a breach in the marriage bond.

It is true that the wife owes obedience to her husband, but he, on his side, is bound to treat her well. The wife is a servant, but not a slave, and her good conduct depends upon the treatment she receives from her husband.

The Englishman, deceived by his wife, says to himself, "If some one had stolen my horse, I should be entitled to damages; now I have a still stronger claim to damages, since it is my wife that I have been robbed of." He pleads before the civil court, and demands monetary compensation from his wife's lover for the "alienation of her affections." The Englishman does not say to himself, "My wife differs from my horse in that she can think, and if she has been unfaithful to me, there is no robbery, since she has not been taken by force, but has acted with her eyes open."

In France, it is the husband of an unfaithful wife who is covered with ridicule, and not she who is covered with shame; and, to explain the error of her conduct, the public looks for defects in him, and seeks excuses for her.

Among the Maoris, when a wife deceives her husband, people say, "If he had treated his wife well, this thing would not have happened;" and until the truth of the matter has been sifted out, the husband is looked askance at. If it is discovered that he has not been a good husband, and that his wife had fair reason to consider herself ill-used, her tribe often takes revenge by making raids on the "pah" to which the husband belongs, and pillaging the huts; and the husband's people admit the justice of the proceeding by allowing themselves to be plundered without trying to defend their belongings, and without even making a complaint.

The Maori does not exact that his *fiancée* should be virtuous, and she very seldom is; but when he has married her, he demands that she shall be faithful to him, and it is very rarely that his conduct to his wife furnishes her with an excuse for going wrong.

When two Maoris are taken *flagrante delicto*, they are tied together and exposed for three days to the insults of their fellow-creatures, who spit on them and subject them to all kinds of ignominy. At the end of three days, they are driven out of the tribe, and the reprisals which I spoke of above take place, if the conduct of the husband toward his wife has given her any ground of excuse for infidelity.

Adultery is an offence keenly felt among the Maoris, and it has often been the cause of desperate fights between different tribes.

The Maoris have a vivid and poetical imagination.

This is how a Maori expressed himself on the beauty of English women:

"Beauty in our women is like a lovely spring day. A squall arises, and all has disappeared. The English women's beauty lasts longer. They are lovely as the morning. Roses are mantling on their cheeks, and the azure of the firmament is reflected in their eyes."

They have some exquisitely poetical legends. The Maoris tell their children that, at the beginning of the world, the Heaven and the Earth were married, but that they were separated by their children, the winds. "Up to this time they have remained separated. Yet their mutual love still continues—the soft warm sighs of her loving bosom still ever rise up to him, ascending from the woody mountains and valleys, and men call these mists; and the vast Heaven, as he mourns through the long nights his separation from his beloved, drops frequent tears upon her bosom, and men, seeing these call them dewdrops." *

The Maori mythology, full as it is of the most poetical and fantastic legends, shows what an imaginative mind this race has always had.

Sir George Grey has collected all these legends and published them in English, and in the Maori language, of which he is a perfect master. This is one of the least of the things that Sir George Grey has done for New Zealand. Late Governor-in-Chief of New Zealand, he is the greatest administrator that England ever sent to her Colonies. His name is still venerated in South Africa, as it is in New Zealand. Arriving in the latter country in most troublous times, the first thing he did

* Sir George Grey's *Polynesian Mythology*.

was to master the Maori language, so as to be able to hear and understand for himself the grievances of the chiefs, and he grew so fond of the people that he has lived among them ever since, ruling over them in a spirit of justice, consideration, conciliation, and moderation. To this day the Maoris swear by him, and look upon him as their guardian angel, although he no longer governs them, but sits in the New Zealand Parliament as an ordinary member, keenly watching over their interests. If England always sent to her Colonies representatives of the stamp of Sir George Grey, her name would be venerated wherever the Union Jack floats.

The Maoris are lazy and proud. They pass their time in sleeping, smoking, and lounging in the sun in a delicious *otium cum dignitate*. In Africa, the aborigines are servants, carters, drovers, errand boys, general handy men; in short, they work for the whites. The Maori does not work for the whites; it is the whites who work for him. Only the women will make themselves useful.

The Maoris are admirably treated by the English, who have left them, in the centre of the North Island, a large territory with undisputed possession, called King's Country. They let their land to the English, and live on their rents, and there is humor in English people having Maoris for landlords. Some of them enjoy large revenues. I heard of one whose income amounted to fifteen thousand pounds a year.

Near Wanganui I saw English workmen making a pirogue for some Maoris, and actually executing Maori carvings, while their dusky employers, voluptuously stretched on the grass smoking their pipes, gave them directions without even taking the trouble to raise themselves.

The Maoris are a licentious people. Their dances are obscene; the carvings with which their houses are ornamented are grossly indecent; their god is Priapus, and their actions and language show that *phallus* is a fixed idea with them.

The *haka*, a madly intoxicating dance, is a saraband where men and women bound and writhe, indulging in all kinds of revolting gestures. I only saw a mild family *haka*, a dance quite anodyne and most proper compared to the veritable *haka*, which I took on trust. Human nature interests me everywhere, and I resign myself to nearly every sight, sound, and even often smell, to get a clearer insight into the ways of the people among whom I happen to be; but there are times when it is necessary to draw the line and not go to extremes, and if there is an extreme in this world it is the Maori *haka*. This dance is now prohibited by the English. In its mad fascination the Maoris lose all self-control, and abandon themselves, in shameless fashion, to the most revolting acts. It is a frightful saturnalia, but has such an irresistible attraction for them that, when once begun, the whole neighborhood pours in and joins in the dance, which continues till exhaustion supervenes.

In a Maori house, in the neighborhood of Wanganui, I had the honor of making the acquaintance of Wic,* in her time a famous Maori belle. She was lying on the floor smoking a pipe. She rose and shook hands with me. The ex-siren is over forty, but still has rem-

* Abbreviation for Victoria.

nants of great beauty. For a long time she led a loose life in the cities, but she has now returned to the fold, and become the docile and faithful wife of a Maori. She smokes her pipe and dreams of youthful triumphs, and her husband is so proud of his bargain that he exempts her from all manual labor. It is related of her that she was one night in the box of a theatre, where gentlemen had taken her to see a troop of Maoris perform. She was attired in European evening-dress. Presently the *haka* begins, but, of course, a very well-behaved one, so as not to shock the audience too much. This does not suit Wic, who thinks the sport rather slow. Moreover, she grows hot with shame and anger at the idea that the *haka* is going on and she is not of it. The sight of the dance, proper and restricted though it be, electrifies her. She cannot stand it any longer. Away with the dress, the corset, and the rest. In the twinkling of an eye she is free. With a bound she leaps onto the stage, leads the dance, and, by her yells and excitement, works the others up to such a pitch of delirium that the audience, horrified and fearful, make for the doors in all haste, leaving Wic and her comrades in full possession to finish their Sabbath.

The *pah*, or Maori village, is a collection of wooden cabins surrounded by a fence, nearly every post of which is surmounted by a grinning manikin in wood, with protruding tongue, crooked legs, hands crossed over the stomach, a huge mouth, and oblique eyes of mother-of-pearl. This horribly grimacing figure reappears on each side and over the door of every cabin.

The house consists of one large square room, the walls and the floor of which are covered with woven matting. The roof descends to the ground on either side, and is arched over the door, pagoda fashion. The interior of the hut is used as a dormitory, where the sexes are divided, as in public baths, *minus* the partition.

Not more than thirty or forty years ago, the Maoris were cannibals; but see how times have changed them! To-day, four Maoris are members of the New Zealand

MAORI PAH.
[*From a Photograph by* BURTON BROS., *Dunedin, New Zealand.*]

Parliament, and one of them is said to have assisted in his youth at cannibal feasts, where the *menu* consisted of human steaks and tit-bits. These Maoris are in Parliament to defend the rights and interests of the natives.

Does not a fact like this help us to understand the success of the undertakings of the firm, John Bull & Co.?

In all parts of New Zealand, even in King's Country, the Maoris go to school, and they shine everywhere by their intelligence. Some of them at present occupy honorable posts in Government offices. But such is the nomadic and wild instinct of the race, that when a Maori is seized with an irresistible impulse to leave the town and revisit his *pah*, he seldom returns.

BUSH CREEK, NEW ZEALAND.
[*From a Photograph by* J. VALENTINE & SON, *Dundee.*]

Drink, contact and intermarriage with the whites, etiolate the Maoris, and in every part of New Zealand except King's Country, where they lead their natural life, their numbers are rapidly decreasing.

Adieu, New Zealand, most beautiful of lands. Often I think of thy poetical legends, and feast my eyes again in imagination on thy lovely landscapes! I would fain enjoy again the hospitality of thy kind inhabitants, and listen to the liquid language of thy natives. I fancy I hear again their melodious *Mokololulu*, *Kirikitata*, *Warakewera*, *Waramanatikipu*.

Good-bye! *Ta-ta!*

CHAPTER XXVII.

From Melbourne to the Cape of Good Hope—The *Australasian*
—Sunday on Board Ship—Conversions—Death of a Poor
Mother—Ceremony—Table Bay—Arrival at Cape Town.

SEVERAL companies send from London to Australia ships which touch at the Cape on the way; but only the Aberdeen liners go from Australia to the Cape; the others continue their route around the world by Cape Horn and Rio Janeiro. There is consequently no choice.

I remember having read in Mr. Froude's interesting *Oceana*, that the great historian had made the voyage from England to Melbourne on board the *Australasian*. Seeing by the papers that this ship was about to sail, I said to myself, "If the *Australasian* is good enough for Mr. Froude, it is certainly good enough for me," and I went forthwith to engage cabins.

The distance from Melbourne to the Cape is about six thousand miles. The *Australasian* does the voyage in twenty-two days. Twenty-two days lost out of one's life, spent in doing nothing; the most monotonous, the most wearisome interval, during which not one glimpse of land is to be had.

Never mind, thought I, I shall utilize those twenty-two days for work.

Work! Alas! man proposes, but the sea indisposes.

And the Sundays! Oh, the Sundays! Even the harmless games that are played on board ship on weekdays are suspended. It would be shocking to play a game of quoits; chess, I suppose, would be criminal. If you were to propose an innocent game of *beggar-my-neighbor*, the passengers would veil their faces in dismay at your boldness. Reading and hymn-singing are the only pastimes tolerated. It is curious the connection there is in some minds between high sanctity and flat music. Those who cannot sing, lounge about the ship and read and yawn away the day, and long for the Monday. We are thirty-two passengers in the saloon. Out of these there are not two who do not express their regrets at having to pass their Sundays thus, but, mind you, there is not one who dares venture to be frank and sincere and to act according to his conscience. It is the fear of the *qu'en dira-t-on* in all its idiocy; it is cowardice pure and simple.

It is impossible to travel on an English boat without having the bore who seeks to convert you, and that before trying to find out whether his victim may not happen to be as good a Christian as he. He was on board the *Australasian*. Every Sunday he held classes in the saloon. He had succeeded in persuading half a dozen passengers to go and hear him read a chapter of the Bible and discuss its contents. He had his own views. Where is the true-born Englishman who has not his own views on theology? It is a craze. I know few Englishmen who would not be able to preach a sermon to their neighbors, and found a new religion.

This good man declared music to be "one of the snares of Satan," and every time we made a little music on deck to enliven our evenings, he kept away. The English nation alone can boast of producing this species, and no nation in the world thinks of being jealous of the production.

Day followed day, and each resembled the one before.

Not a single incident to break the monotony of the three weeks' passage.

Or rather, yes, there was one, and a very pathetic one, too.

We had among the second-class passengers a gentle old woman of over seventy, the mother of two married daughters, one living at the Cape, the other in Australia. Having lost her husband, the good soul had realized the little money at her disposal and had gone to her daughter at the Cape to seek a home with her. This daughter had sent her on to the sister in Australia, but the poor woman was not to find rest there. Her son-in-law would none of her, and she had been fain to embark for the Cape again to see if daughter number one would not give her shelter for her remaining days.

Struck with apoplexy, she died in mid-ocean. The previous Sunday I had noticed her at divine service, dressed in her best, and looking almost happy. Her corpse was sewn up in canvas, covered with the Union Jack, and brought on deck. Surrounded by passengers and crew, the captain read the burial service, and at the moment where the words, "I commit thy body to the deep," were substituted for, "Dust to dust and ashes to ashes," the boat stopped steam, and the sailors, who retained the body by cords, lowered it into the sea amid impressive silence. The boat, having deposited its burden in the ocean, steamed ahead again. The dead woman's purse contained two shillings and sevenpence half-penny, and the daughter she wanted to join at the Cape lived sixty miles from Cape Town!

The poor mother had found rest, and there was no need now for her children to trouble about her; at last they were rid of that useless piece of furniture which the lower-class English call mother.

A few flying-fish, from time to time a school of porpoises, once or twice a whale—beyond that nothing. The blue sky overarching the blue sea.

At last, on the 2d of April, 1893, we sighted the coast of Africa, and soon we were following it pretty closely from Algoa Bay to Table Bay, in which nestles Cape Town, the capital of Cape Colony.

Before entering Table Bay, we passed Danger Point, where in 1852 the transport ship *Birkenhead* came to grief and sank, while the soldiers on board, seeing death inevitable, said "Good-bye" to the world by singing "God Save the Queen."

I do not know any town more picturesquely situated than Cape Town. The houses are dotted over an area of four or five miles, at the foot of three mountains, the central one of which stands up four thousand feet into the air, and has a breadth of two miles at the top. The summit of this, Table Mountain, is an immense plateau, which, seen from the sea, is perfectly horizontal. Often it is covered with clouds that spread over its surface and fall on either side, giving just the appearance of a white tablecloth. It looks as if the table were spread for some Titan of those parts.

The clouds have melted, the sun goes down in a bed of gold, throwing its fires on every corner of the panorama. An hour later, the moon inundates the scene with her ghostly light. The engines are stopped, and the boat lies in the offing, ready to continue her journey to-morrow.

Not a sound reaches our ears as we lie at anchor. Only the thousands of lights glittering in the town remind us that we are among our fellow-creatures once more.

We shall land to-morrow morning.

CHAPTER XXVIII.

Anglo-Dutch—John Bull, Charged with the Care of the Cape for the Prince of Orange, Keeps it for Himself—Mixture of Races—Cape Town—The Town and its Environs—Paarl—The Huguenots—Stellenbosch—Happy Folk—Drapers' Assistants—Independence a Characteristic Feature of the South Africans.

South Africa is composed of two English colonies, one of which, Cape Colony, is very Dutch; of two independent Dutch republics, which are perfectly English; of several territories, such as Bechuanaland, Mashonaland, Zululand, Pondoland, Basutoland, Nyassaland, Matabeleland, and of a few other little lands protected by the firm, John Bull & Co.

At the beginning of the century the Cape was still a Dutch colony, but the English, fearing that Napoleon, who had just placed his brother Louis on the throne of Holland, might make use of the Cape to possess himself of India, installed themselves there in 1806 to take care of it for the Prince of Orange, dethroned by Buonaparte.

Now, one of John Bull's mottoes is that of the late Marshal MacMahon, "*J'y suis, j'y reste*"—Here I am, and here I stay. He was in the Cape, and he stayed there. You would more easily withdraw a lump of butter from a dog's mouth than John Bull from the territory where he has installed himself.

The colony was definitely ceded to the English in 1815 by the Treaty of Paris.

Many old Dutch families are still to be found in the principal towns of the south of the colony, but the active Dutch element, the farmers, must have steadily retired northward as the English advanced. These Dutchmen, now known as Boers, went and founded the Orange Free State and the Transvaal, or South African Republic; but now they cannot very well go any farther, for the English have just taken possession of Matabeleland, and the circle is made: the Boers are now completely surrounded, at the south by the Cape, on the west by Bechuanaland, on the north by Mashonaland and Matabeleland, and on the east by Natal, Zululand, and a Portuguese territory, which the English will never allow them to acquire, even if the Portuguese should ever be willing to sell it, for this territory contains Delagoa Bay, the only harbor of South Africa.

What is the political future of the Boers, that handful of people, antiquated and stubborn, but brave and patriotic, who occupy a country emboweled with gold? We may be able to answer the question presently. An interesting interview with President Kruger will help us. But let us stay a moment in the Cape.

The South African Colonies differ essentially from those of Australasia. The latter are purely British, and, with the exception of the Maoris of New Zealand, the native population is little seen, save in skeleton form, adorning the museums of the large towns. In South Africa, the white population is mixed, British and Dutch; and the colored population, far from being extinct, seems everywhere to be full of life, an African and Asiatic population, ranging from the ebony black of the Zulus to the rich olive of the Malays: Hottentots, Kaffirs, Zulus, Fingos, Pondos, Basutos, etc.

I like Cape Town, with its old Dutch houses, the animation of its streets, the splendor of its public buildings, its Parliament, its gardens, its picturesque environs, its refined society, its Malay population—whose women look like Madonnas adorned for a great church procession.

Every day I used to go and feast my eyes on a su-

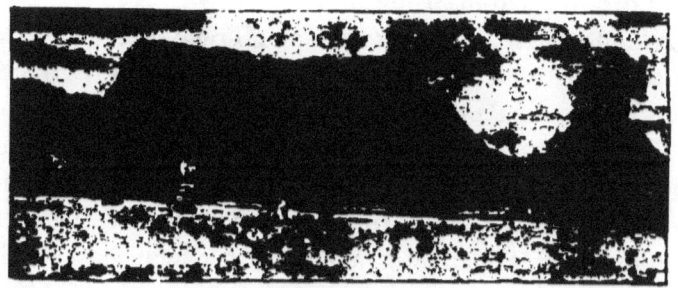

TABLE MOUNTAIN.

perb view. Taking up a position at the end of Adderley Street, I had, on the right, the Museum and the Botanical Gardens; in front, an immense avenue of centenary oaks; on the left, the Parliament; and, as a background for the whole, Table Mountain, which seemed to almost overhang the landscape. I could never tire my eyes of this magnificent sight.

A drive that I shall never forget is one that I took in company with the late M. Joseph Perrette, French consul at the Cape, and several friends. We first passed through the fashionable suburbs of Newland

and Claremont, which are scattered over with lovely villas, set in a veritable forest of oaks and eucalyptus; then we saw the smiling plains of Constantia, celebrated for the good wine they produce; from thence we went through a delightfully undulating country to Houts Bay, where, under a blue sky and a genial sun, we lunched in the garden of a family of Kaffirs. After that, following the contour of the mountain, we re-entered Cape Town by the Victoria Road. I do not know Sorrento, but I can scarcely believe that it can be possible to take a lovelier drive than the one we took around Table Mountain.

About twenty miles from Cape Town there are two most picturesque and interesting little towns, perfectly Dutch, named Paarl and Stellenbosch.

Paarl (Pearl) is composed of a single street seven miles in length, at the foot of a mountain range, along a narrow valley. This town is the cradle of the Afrikander-Bond, a patriotic association which has for its object the future emancipation of South Africa. It was here, too, that a number of Huguenots took up their abode in the beginning of last century. The De Villiers, the Duplessis, the Du Toits, the Leroux, are everywhere; they fill the highest and the most lowly posts; a pious population, peaceful, intelligent, and hard-working. Those descendants of the Huguenots, victims of the Revocation of the Edict of Nantes, I have seen them in England, in Holland, in America, everywhere the same. It was the cream of France which was obliged to leave the country in 1685 that Madame de Maintenon might become a king's wife. These Huguenots are completely lost to France.

Those I met in Africa not only speak no word of French, but they do not even know how to pronounce their own names.

I was lunching one day on board the *Scot*, the finest and fastest boat which plies between England and South Africa. Many notabilities of Cape Town had been invited. The director of the company whispered to me, "There is the Chief-Justice of the colony. I will introduce you to him; his name is Sir Henry di Filchi."

"Di Filchi," I replied; "how do you spell the name?"

"V-i-l-l-i-e-r-s," he said.

"You don't say so!" I exclaimed; "and that makes Filchi? Can it be possible?"

This is how it came about.

When those Huguenots took refuge in Holland, and from thence went and settled in the Cape, then a Dutch colony, they found a tyrannical government that forbade them to speak French, or teach it to their children. At the end of fifty years they had become Dutch; to-day they are British subjects, but their hearts are more Dutch than English. As for France, they have completely forgotten it. Alas! what do they owe to France, who ignominiously chased them from her shores?

If you go to Canada, you will find a French population that has been subject to Great Britain for a hundred and fifty years past, but these have remained French in heart. Not only do they continue to speak French, but they do not, and will not, speak anything else. I mean the masses, of course. John Bull leaves them alone. He says to them, "Speak what you please, worship God as you will;" and those French Catholics of the seventeenth century have remained French and Catholic, so that to visit them is to visit the France of two hundred years ago.

This is a fact which, among a thousand others, has explained to me the success of the English. They are past masters in diplomacy. The governing hand is firm, but wears a velvet glove. They seem to say, "Do not mind us, make yourself at home." But John Bull is there all the time.

The town of Paarl received its name from a rock situated on the top of the mountain, which is said to resemble pearl when the sun strikes it. I was quite willing to believe it, and even went so far as to see it; and if you wish to please the Paarl people, I advise you to do the same. As in the case of the Southern Cross, faith is a great help.

There are skeptics who believe because they see; there are more accommodating people who see because they believe.

If every town in the world should take part in a revolution, Paarl and her neighbor Stellenbosch would be the very last to join. Nothing more peaceful could be conceived than these two pretty little towns. Hardly a creature in the streets. About three o'clock a few people indulge in a sedate, slow walk.

Stellenbosch is embowered in oaks which were brought from Europe, and flourish in this climate like the proverbial green bay. Every street is an avenue, a cathedral nave of green leafiness which the sun scarcely penetrates. Along the streets, on either side, runs a stream in which the housewife does the family wash.

The snow-white houses with their orange-colored shutters are quite picturesque. Outdoor foot-gear must be taken off at the door, I should think, as in Holland. The bright colors, the luxuriant greenery, the eternal blue sky, make up a delicious picture of calm and repose.

From twelve to two, the shops of Paarl and Stellenbosch are closed. The worthy shopkeepers are dining and taking a siesta, and as their customers are doing the same, trade in no wise suffers. What a contrast to those feverish Americans who at one o'clock put up on their door, "Gone to dinner; back in five minutes." Ah, my good De Villiers, Duplessis, and Du Toits, how sensible of you! Five minutes for dinner, what folly! Take your time, let digestion proceed quietly, and you will die of old age. And to live long and happily, is not that the great desideratum with most people? Life is only given to us once; let us make the best of it while we have the chance—we shall never get another.

I admire the independence of the South African shopkeepers.

The day after my arrival in Cape Town, I discovered that my stock of handkerchiefs was getting small. I went to a draper's shop, and, as politely as I could, asked the assistant to show me some new ones. When the purchase was made, I said to him:

"Will you please get them marked for me?"

"What do you take me for?" he replied; "cannot you get some ink and mark them yourself?"

There was no rudeness in the expression of his face, nor in the tone of his voice. He was right. Could I not buy marking ink and do the thing myself?

"It is not a service that I ask you," I rejoined; "I am willing to pay for your trouble."

"It is not done anywhere, sir."

"I beg your pardon," said I; "it is done in France and England, for instance; but perhaps you never heard of those countries?"

"Well, yes, I have heard of them; but I can't say that I exactly know where they are."

It was stupid of me to be offended. I ought to have shown appreciation of the young man's independence by buying his handkerchiefs. I went to another shop near by, instead.

I related the incident to a journalist who came to interview me in the afternoon. Later on, I saw the matter commented on in the press, and amongst other remarks, the following: "The man in the Cape Town store who brusquely replied to Max O'Rell's request to have some handkerchiefs marked, 'Do it yourself!' was unconsciously presenting to this student of national characteristics the text and keynote to a whole treatise on South Africa."

Independence, then, is a characteristic trait here. I am delighted at that; it is a very excellent trait. I hate servility—but I do love politeness.

CHAPTER XXIX.

The Dutch Puritans—The "Doppers"—A Case of Conscience—The Afrikander-Bond—Its Relations with John Bull—Tickets at Reduced Price—John Bull Lies Low—"God Save the Queen" in the South African Republic.

THE nations that John Bull has conquered have generally received the Bible in exchange for their territory. The Dutch received nothing in exchange for South Africa. They were more religious, more Protestant, than the English, and they are so still. As Puritans they outdo the Scotch, and even the austerity of the followers of John Knox cannot be compared with that of the Dutch Reformed Church. Not content with this Reformed Church, the Cape Dutchmen and the Boers of the interior have started a dissenting church still more strict and austere, whose members have received the name of "Doppers." To these good people music is sinful, and their monotonous chants in church are not accompanied. They object to hymns and canticles. They sing verses of the Bible at the rate of one word per minute, each word dying away like the note of a crow in distress. These Dutch Reformed churches dominate the English ones throughout South Africa, and the English population, to avoid the possibility of the Dutch outdoing them in the matter of piety, often join in the Dopper devotions.

The Doppers are as practical as they are pious, aud when they have to decide a case of conscience, they do it in a manner favorable to their interests.

For example, in their eyes dancing is a mortal sin, but although they let their halls for lectures and concerts, they never let them for balls—without doubling the price of hire. So much for the hall, so much for soothing their conscience. It is just what the Scotch cab-drivers do in Edinburgh and Glasgow on Sunday—double their fare. John Bull has nothing to teach the Dutch.

The English and the Dutch at the Cape would do very well without each other, but they live in peace and co-operate honorably in the development of the colony. It is true that the Parliament is opened by the High Commissioner in the name of the Queen of England, whom he represents; but autonomy is so complete, that the Dutch feel themselves as free as if they enjoyed that perfect independence which they hope one day to obtain—by purely constitutional means, of course. At present they form the Conservative element in politics, and support the Afrikander Bond. This association calmly pursues its aim, and not a single member would think of taking up a gun to hasten its realization. It succeeds in making the Ministry do pretty much what it wishes without giving umbrage to the Queen's representative. Its chief, Mr. J. H. Hofmeyr, plays in this colonial Parliament the part which the late Mr. Parnell played in the House of Commons—the friend or the enemy who must be always taken into account.

The members of the Afrikander-Bond hold, with the greatest impunity, meetings, at which they express their hopes in the frankest terms. What does the Government do? What does it do? It sends policemen to these meetings. To arrest the orators and hale them before a tribunal for high treason? Not at all; to protect orators and audience, and to assure them of their right to give their opinions in public, even when one of those opinions may be, "that John Bull be turned out and the independence of the South African Colonies proclaimed." And that which best shows how little John Bull's yoke makes itself felt in the Colonies, is perhaps the following incident, which always seemed to me extremely piquant and full of British humor. When the delegates of the Afrikander-Bond wish to go by train to take part in some meeting, held in the provinces by one of the branches of this patriotic but revolutionary association, the Minister of Railways* gives them tickets at reduced fares. In presence of facts like these, the Dutch have a right to call themselves perfectly independent.

Thus, you see for yourself, John Bull "lies low" all the time. And yet there he is. He advances by small steps, but they are sure ones; and the English language makes such progress, that in the free library at Burghersdorp, one of the most Dutch towns of the Cape, I found two thousand English volumes and about forty Dutch books.

There is something so fascinating in the English education, that the young, who thrive and expand in its liberty, get anglicized at school, whatever their nationality may be. English education, that is what makes proselytes for England. How many Frenchmen in London have said to me, with a sad sigh, "These

---

* The railways at the Cape belong to the Government, and are administered by a Minister, as in Australasia.

English schools *corrupt* my boys, and I do not see how I am to keep them French."

The young Dutch boys at the Cape play foot-ball and cricket, and get anglicized at school.

But in this line the most striking thing I saw was at Johannesburg, the most important town of the Transvaal, that perfectly independent South African Republic. When, at the end of a concert, the orchestra plays the national hymn of the Transvaal, no one pays any attention, and the audience talks and remains seated; but the moment the first notes of "God Save the Queen" are struck, every one rises, and all the men's heads are uncovered, so that you really ask yourself whether here also you are not in one of the branches of the firm, John Bull & Co.

CHAPTER XXX.

Mr. Rhodes, Premier of Cape Colony—The Man—His Work—His Aim.

ABOUT twenty-five years ago, a boy of fifteen, considered by English doctors to be in the last stage of consumption, set out for the Cape, not with the idea of being cured, but to prolong his existence by a few months. The unique climate of South Africa cured him. The boy is now a man of forty, in perfect health, a millionaire twice over, Premier of the colony, the indispensable man in South Africa—and his name is Cecil John Rhodes.

HON. CECIL RHODES.
[*From a Photograph in the possession of the Editor of "South Africa."*]

Mr. Rhodes is six feet high. His head is large and powerful looking, his eye is dreamy but observant. He has the quizzical look of a cynic, and the large forehead of an enthusiast.

When he laughs, which is not often, the left cheek shows a dimple that you would think charming in a child or a young woman. The face is placid; it is that of a diplomatist who knows how to wait and see what you are going to say or do. All suddenly this face lights up, and the gaze becomes resolute; it is the face of a man of action, who knows how to seize an occasion and turn it to account. His dress is *negligé*, and his hat impossible.

MR. RHODES' HOUSE.

I have seen him go to the Parliament House in a gray cut-away coat, and go into his room to put on the black frock-coat which is *de rigueur* for the colonial members. The sitting over, the black coat is put away in its cupboard. Prigs take offence at his free-and-easy ways. There is a story that he was once present at the opening of a new railway line. The station happened to be by the sea. In the middle of the ceremony, all at once, Mr. Rhodes is missed, and every one wonders what has become of him. Suddenly some one espies, a hundred yards off, the figure of the Premier, *en Apollon*, coming out of the sea and going towards his clothes, which he had left on the beach whilst he took a dip.

Opportunist *par excellence*, Mr. Rhodes serves John Bull and the Afrikander-Bond, and takes care that they both serve him. His ambition is to acquire for the mother-country all the South African land as far as the Zambesi. If John Bull gives him a free hand, this will be realized, and Mr. Rhodes will be Prime Minister of an English colony larger than all Europe. If John Bull hampers him, and busies himself too much about that which, according to Mr. Rhodes, concerns him very little, you may one day hear of an independent African Confederation, with Mr. Rhodes for President and Mr. Hofmeyr for Vice-President.

Whatever happens, you will certainly hear of Mr. Rhodes.

CHAPTER XXXI.

South African Towns—The Hotels—The Usefulness of the Moon—Kaffirland—Kimberley—The Diamond Mines—The De Beers Company—A Week's Find—Life in the "Compounds"—A Disagreeable Week before Going to buy Wives.

JUST as in America, Australia, and all new countries, there is terrible monotony for the eye in South Africa. Describe one little town and you have described all. You do not find money squandered on public buildings as in Australia : that is because the Dutch element acts as a curb to English push and improvidence. Every town has its market-place, in Dutch fashion—an immense square, where the Reformed church generally stands, and where the Cape wagons, veritable houses on wheels, drawn by oxen, and conducted by Kaffirs armed with a whip ten yards long, make halt. No walks, and very few walkers. A few negresses doing the street scavenging with their hands, gathering up the excrement of the oxen, and carrying it away on trays borne on the head to their houses, where, when dried, it serves to make fires. Some old Dopper, who has just risen from his siesta, walks with slow tread and suns himself.

With the exception of Kimberley, which is lighted by electricity, and Cape Town and Port Elizabeth, which are lighted by gas, the towns are nearly all lighted by lamps. A few towns, such as Worcester, George Town, very pretty and picturesque places, depend upon the moon. No moon, no light, and people stay at home. As in Australia, no drainage.

All this strikes one with astonishment after a visit to America, where little holes of a hundred inhabitants are lighted by electricity.

And yet the country is not asleep. It advances with rapid strides, and business flourishes.

The hotels all resemble one another, and so do the bills of fare, except that a few are worse than the others. Everywhere the same routine. At six o'clock in the morning, the nigger knocks at your door. You have to rouse yourself, and rise to open the door to him. He places on your night-table a cup of atrocious coffee, which I advise you to take as you would a dose of castor oil, toss it off quick and do not think about it. After that, you get under the bed coverings again, and believe that you are going to be left in peace. Sweet but short-lived illusion. At half-past six the negro returns. You are obliged to get up again and reopen the door to him. He comes to fetch the cup. Useless to tell him the night before that you do not take coffee in bed. That is no business of his. He has his routine to go through, and, to carry it out, he has the intelligence and the fidelity of a French sentinel.

As in America and Australia, if your neighbor at table takes you for a stranger in the land, he cannot resist the temptation of asking you the eternal question, "Well, sir, and what do you think of South Africa?"

Here, as in Australia and New Zealand, the important towns are on the seaboard—Cape Town, Port Elizabeth, East London, Durban. Port Elizabeth has a great commercial importance, and the future of East London is assured. All these towns are now in direct communication with the diamond mines of Kimberley and the gold mines of Johannesburg. In a few months Durban will be so connected also.

There are two towns that I would advise the traveler not to miss—King Williamstown, a pretty place embowered in verdure, and a veritable hive of activity, and Grahamstown, the city of saints, inhabited by 16,000

Street in Kimberley

human beings perfectly petrified, and lighted by a few paraffin lamps as sleepy as the inhabitants. But it is the journey that I recommend more particularly: about eighty miles' driving to do across that most interesting country, the centre of Kaffirland. You pass through groups of kraals, where the natives continue to live as if no white man had ever yet set foot on African soil.

The last eighteen miles or so before reaching Grahamstown present a series of enchantments. The country becomes wild and hilly. You enter Pluto's Valley, along the bottom of which you pass between steep and wooded crags, peopled with large baboons, which gambol around you, or, perched on a tree or the edge of a rock, calmly look down on you from the height of their grandeur. Add to that, at about six o'clock in the evening, a marvelous sunset. You will arrive in town shaken, stiff, bruised, famishing, and enchanted with your day's journey.

It would be out of place in a book like this to describe the towns. The reader who wishes to obtain precise information about the population, the commerce, and resources of such and such a town in South Africa, will find them in the numerous guides at his disposition. We study life everywhere, and commerce statistics are not much in our line.

But we must halt a little at Kimberley, whose diamond industry has been the saving of Cape Colony.

With the exception of a few streets graced by pretty villas, Kimberley is a town built of brown mud in the midst of a desert. Its market-place is the vastest in the colony, but it is surrounded by tumble-down buildings, which give it a pitiful air of desolation. At Kimberley you will search in vain for anything but diamonds; but as this search has been so fruitful that all the companies have been obliged to amalgamate so as to regulate the production and prevent these precious stones from becoming too common, Kimberley deserves a visit, and there are happy people to be seen there.

Before going to the mines, and to show you that Kimberley is not an adventurers' camp, but a town inhabited by intelligent people who read and study, I must make mention of the public library, one of the largest and best stocked that I saw in the Colonies, and which possesses about fifteen hundred volumes in the French language, representing all that is best in our literature, from the poetry of Malherbe to the novels of M. Alphonse Daudet.

Twenty years ago, a young negro, serving on a farm situated between the Vaal and the Orange River, found a little white stone, which he showed one day to a traveler passing through those parts. The traveler bought the little stone, and sold it for £500. It was the first Kimberley diamond. The news got abroad, and a crowd soon invaded the borders of the Vaal. They sought and they found. In twenty-three years Kimberley has yielded diamonds which have been sold in the rough for the fabulous sum of £35,000,000. The lovely Countess of Dudley possesses a diamond, called the "Star of South Africa," valued at £25,000.

A few weeks before my visit to Kimberley, there had been found a diamond of four hundred and twenty-eight carats. The De Beers Company sold it to an Indian prince for the pretty little sum of £15,000.

Companies have been started in the neighborhood, riches have been reaped, and Cape Colony, which twenty years ago was at a very low ebb, now enjoys the greatest opulence. A few years later, Johannesburg, with its gold mines, completed the fortune of this land, which compensates for the aridity of its surface by the wealth that lies underneath. Africa will lack bread and water before it lacks gold and diamonds.

KIMBERLEY MARKET-PLACE.

Under the guidance of Mr. Gardner F. Williams, an American, the general manager, I visited the subterranean mines of De Beers and Kimberley; and near by I plunged my eyes into the depths of a pit, the surface of which is twenty acres and the depth three hundred feet. In this pit negroes, like a swarm of black ants, dug and threw the precious mud into the tumbrils, which went off and emptied their contents into machines. When the sand is sifted, it is sent to sheds and placed on tables, where workmen, under the surveillance of lynx-eyed watchers, search for diamonds with little rakes, and throw them into locked tin boxes.

These boxes are sent under escort to the office of the company, and there the diamonds are spread out and classed by experts, according to their size, color, and purity. These different groups are placed on tissue paper on a table, where I saw over £200,000 worth. This was the find of the four preceding days. They were of all shades—white, yellow, brownish, some reddish-white, others opaque, others of a bluish-gray. The yellow ones, it appears, are much sought after by the Turks and Indian rajahs, while the Americans are the best customers of the company for white diamonds.

But that which interested me most at Kimberley was the life led by the miners, in whom were represented all the tribes of South Africa—Kaffirs, Zulus, Pondos, Fingos, Basutos, Hottentots, etc.

The negro who works in the mines accepts a contract which makes him the prisoner of the company during the time his engagement lasts; but the good negro is delighted with his lot. He has fresh air, good food, and amusements. If he is ill, he is well looked after, and at the end of a year he has in his leather belt, which serves him for a purse, from sixty to eighty pounds with which to buy oxen, and with these oxen to buy wives who will work for him, and allow him to pass his life in the softest of *far nientes*. So, to attain this end, he joyfully accepts a year of imprisonment. He will sometimes even walk five hundred miles to reach Kimberley, and try and get enrolled. How many poor whites do I know who would consent to a year of imprisonment without dishonor, to live on their means for the rest of their lives! The miners are lodged, or rather barracked, in great enclosures called " compounds," which communicate with the entrance to the mines. The "compound" is an immense square, surrounded by iron sheds, where the miners live in sets. They are grouped according to the tribe to which they belong. The centre forms a large court, several acres in size, where they amuse themselves by day. They cannot have any communication with outsiders, and, to prevent the possibility of their throwing diamonds over the roofs, the whole compound is covered in with close wire netting.

Accompanied by the manager and several officials of the De Beers Company, I went into the court, visited the sheds and the hospital, and I can say that, having seen everywhere that crowd of negroes, laughing, amusing themselves, and all looking resplendent with health, I came out of the "compound" with the conviction that I had been looking at people who were happy and satisfied with their lot.

One "compound" is occupied by two thousand men; the other by nearly three thousand.

Peacefulness and order reign in the two great "compounds" at Kimberley. The only quarrels that ever arise are tribal ones, childish quarrels that are quelled by a gesture from the superintendent.

When the miners are not on duty, they are free to do what they like. They play cards, dance, sing, give themselves up to trivial merrymakings, do their cooking amicably *en famille*, and as I said before, pass the time in the happiest fashion.

As you see, every precaution is taken that no diamond may escape the company.

The only semblance of cruelty to which these good blacks, who are just like children, are submitted, is the régime they are compelled to live under for the last week of their engagement. But they are warned of this: one of the clauses of the contract which they agree to before entering the service of the company, gives them in detail the description of the treatment they will have to undergo before being set at liberty.

For one week they have to live naked, and in complete imprisonment, not being allowed any communication with their comrades of the "compound." They have to wear hard leather fingerless gloves of enormous dimensions, which prevent them from using their hands, and oblige them to take their nourishment like four-footed animals. Their belongings are taken away and searched, and during that week they have but a blanket belonging to the company to cover them. Their bodies are examined in every part, and never was this expression used with stricter exactness. Their teeth even are examined; and if they have swallowed some precious stone, the gloves prevent the possibility of their handling it to swallow it again. In fact, every precaution that it was possible to think of has been adopted ; and when this week of incarceration is finished, and the negroes have left the " compound " to return to their homes, the company is pretty certain that not one diamond has been stolen.

CHAPTER XXXII.

The Country—The "Veld"—The Plateaus—The Climate—The South African Animals—The Ant-hills—The South Coast—Natal—Durban, the Prettiest Town in South Africa—Zulus and Coolies.

IN South Africa the land is scarcely more clothed than the natives who inhabit it. When you have traveled north for a few hours, all vegetation disappears: no more trees, no more shrubs. The grass grows on the earth and on the sides of the mountains as the hair grows on the head of the Kaffirs, in little tufts here and there.

In spite of this nakedness, the land has in its very desolation a grandeur and a beauty of its own. Thanks to the blue sky, it is not at all sad-looking. It is an original style of beauty, and if you are only careful to start from the principle that it is not necessary for a landscape to resemble Devonshire in order to be beautiful, you will easily admire those that South Africa has to show. From the tops of the highest plateaus you get views that root you to the spot with admiration. In its own line, nothing grander could be conceived than that infinite stretch of *veld*, scattered with flat-topped mountains of different heights, which give to the scene an appearance of a great ocean in a fury.

And the climate in winter! I saw nothing but blue sky for four months; the air was pure and bracing, the atmosphere dry and charged with ozone; a climate in which a person with only half a lung may fairly expect to die of old age like the strongest. And thus one sees numbers of Englishmen who have come and buried themselves in little villages, where they are dying of ennui. But they had rather die of ennui than of consumption. And they are right; to bury oneself in an African village is better than to be buried in Europe,

THE VELD.

you know where. To live anywhere at any cost, so that he lives, is man's motto.

The ideal climate of Africa allows you to undertake things which you would not think of undertaking in any other country. Interminable journeys in trains, in mule or ox wagons, will be powerless to rob you of health or good humor. A sound night's sleep invariably disperses all traces of fatigue. You were so jolted and shaken in the wagon the day before, that you felt yourself all over on alighting, to see what had become of the various portions of your anatomy; but when morning comes, you are fresh and active, ready to start again.

Traveling in South Africa no longer presents any dangers. The natives have accepted their fate, and no longer attack white people. The wild animals have retired northward as civilization advanced, and now one must go as far as Mashonaland to find lions, elephants, buffaloes, and all the big game of Africa. Tartarin would find no more lions at the Cape, in Natal, or in the Transvaal, than he found in the suburbs of Algiers. You find a few leopards, monkeys, antelopes, and gazelles, but that is all. The antelope may still be shot in the neighborhood of almost all the towns at the Cape. These creatures are the prettiest of the inhabitants of South Africa: graceful animals with soft brown eyes, fantastic and symmetrical horns, they present themselves under the most varied forms. The most curious is the *oryx gazella*, or gem-bok, whose parallel and perfectly straight horns are a yard and a half long. The *oryx gazella* is the only one the lion is afraid of. When it is attacked it lowers its head, and its adversary runs the risk of being spiked. His majesty Leo, in his wisdom, thinks twice before venturing.

The museums of the principal towns contain the complete collection of African antelopes. The finest private collection is in the club at Kimberley.

Ostriches in the wild state are now rarely met with in South Africa, but the country abounds with farms where these bipeds are reared in innumerable quantities for the sake of their feathers.

But on the *veld*, nothing: no animals, no vegetation.

To find wooded country, you have to go as far as Bechuanaland. The buildings are of stone, of brick, or of mud, like those of the ancient Celts. Wire is used for fencing, and the excrement of oxen for fires.

The South African desert is hardly inhabited now except by ants. At a certain distance you catch sight of what you suppose to be the huts of a kraal or village of the natives. They are ant-hills, varying in height from three to six feet. There are some which attain a height of twelve and even fifteen feet. These ant-hills are hermetically closed with earth, and present a perfectly even surface, covering a quantity of cells and galleries. Every ant remembers its address more easily than a New Yorker who lives at 1934 One Hundred and Forty-ninth Street, West.

If you scrape the surface of an ant-hill, or make a hole in it, the little yellow ants will come out by thousands, and prove very aggressive. Others will go and tell their neighbors in the lower stories, and presently the whole population will appear and entirely cover the mound.

They will abandon their invaded home, and go to seek a new site, where in a few weeks they will have built with prodigious activity another ant-hill, just like the one that you demolished or simply injured.

I should be sorry to convey the impression that South Africa has no pretty scenery, for the whole south coast, from Cape Town to Natal, is a succession of beautiful landscapes. The forest of Knysna, the district of Oudtshoorn, with its passes, its caves, its interesting ostrich farms, the Buffalo River, at East London, with its hills wooded to the water's edge, reminding one of the Eng-

lish Dart or a miniature Rhine, and, above all, Durban,
the prettiest and most coquettish town in the South African Colonies, with its massive but graceful Town-hall,
its beautiful public gardens, its hills scattered over with
elegant villas set in sub-tropical vegetation. And what
a contrast to the eternal monotony of the *veld!* what
wealth of color! Indians in picturesque costumes,

TOWN-HALL, DURBAN.

Zulus dressed in white tunics bordered with red, living
and moving under a clear blue sky, beside the intense
blue water backed by green hills.

Durban is a feast for the eyes, a *mignardise*.

That which adds greatly to the pleasure of a stay in
Durban is the excellence of the Royal Hotel, by far the
best hostelry in South Africa. It is built around a

courtyard full of palms and ferns, among which fountains play; the cooking is excellent, and the service done by Indian coolies, whose thoughtful attentions

NATAL SCENERY.

are a treat after the independent manners of the colonial or German gentlemen who act as waiters in South African, as well as in American and Australian hotels.

What a sad figure they cut, those poor, emaciated,

lanky Indians, by the side of the Zulus, who are the personification of health and strength! What a limp, nerveless race! As one looks at them, it becomes easy to understand how John Bull made the conquest of India.

In the outskirts of Durban you see the places where these Indians dwell, tumbledown shanties which the most wretched and poorest Connaught peasant would hesitate to lodge his pigs in. Outside, in the sun, sit these miserable creatures, dirty and abject-looking; women with men's heads in their laps searching among their lords' locks, monkey fashion. The children scratch their backs against the doorposts, while their parents scratch their heads. Most of the animation of these people comes from parasitic suggestion on the surface. The more industrious of them work on the sugar and

RAILWAY STATION, VERULAM, NATAL.
[*From a Photograph by* H. S. ELLERBECK, *Natal.*]

tea plantations that abound in South Natal. Others are domestics.

A few Parsees, rich merchants and tradesmen of the town, fat and flourishing, clothed in long gold-embroidered raiment, form a curious contrast to the poor half-clad coolies, whom you see hawking a few bananas at the railway stations, and patronized chiefly by some chattering, merry Zulus, who are installing themselves in high glee in one of the third-class carriages provided in this country for the colored people.

CHAPTER XXXIII.

The Natives of South Africa—First Disappointment—Natives in a Natural State—Scenes of Savage Life—The Kraals—Customs—The Women—Types—Among the Kaffirs and the Zulus—Zulus in "Undress"—I Buy a Lady's Costume, and Carry it off in my Pocket—What Strange Places Virtue Hides in—The Missionaries Gone to the Wrong Place.

IT will take me some time to forget the cruel disappointment I felt on making my first visit to a kraal. It was at Port Elizabeth. I had not yet pushed into the interior, and had only seen civilized savages. I expressed to M. Chabaud, French consul in Port Elizabeth, a wish to see a kraal. "That is very easy," he said; "two or three miles from here we have one, and next Sunday, if you like, we will go and see it. Most of the Kaffirs who belong to this kraal work in the town all the week, but on Sunday you will see them in their natural state." With what pleasure I accepted the proposal! I should see real savages at last.

My visit to the kraal lasted five minutes. I found the "savages" singing Wesleyan hymns, while the small fry played at ball, and whistled that all-pursuing air, "Tararaboomdeay," which for two years I had not been able to get away from. Decidedly I had not gone far enough yet.

Most of the towns in South Africa have near them a kraal, called a *location*, where the Kaffirs employed in the town as porters, carters, servants, etc., live in huts. But in the interior of Cape Colony and Natal, in the

Transvaal and in Zululand, I studied the natives a little, and by the aid, sometimes of Kaffirs and Zulus who spoke a little English, or some English people who spoke Kaffir or Zulu, I was able to gather some interesting facts in talking to them.

A kraal is composed of several huts, generally set upon an eminence which commands a view of the surrounding country.

The hut is built in hive form: poles set in a circle, and flexible rods running horizontally around, the whole perfectly closed by means of earth and branches; one single opening allows the air to penetrate, and the tenants of the hut to enter and leave their residence with a stoop. It is there that they eat, sleep, and pass their time, chattering like magpies. I have seen as many as twenty of them in a hut, the diameter of which at the base was certainly not four yards, the old, the young, the babies, all swarm together with dogs, fowls, and other creatures more closely domestic and of much smaller dimensions, which I need not particularize. A sickly smell of rancid fat, which the bodies of all the South African natives exhale, mixed with the smell of wood smoke, tobacco smoke, and food together, make a composite perfume which it in not in my power to describe. There are odors which, to have an idea of, you must have smelt for yourself.

I passed a whole day in a kraal, living like the Kaffirs whose guest I was. I lunched and dined off mealies and fruit. The bill of fare was not recherché, my table companions had not precisely Mayfair manners, but, on the whole, it was more interesting than dining out in London.

All these good folk seem happy. Children of the sun, they pass their lives frolicking and showing their beautiful white teeth. The women, less playful, attend to all the needs of the family.

Of all the domestic animals invented for the service of man in South Africa, the most useful is woman. There are few offices she is not called upon to fill. I

TRIAL OF NATIVE OUTSIDE COURT OF JUSTICE AT A ZULU LOCATION, NATAL.
[*From a Photograph by* H. S. ELLERBECK, *Natal.*]

have seen these women with a large pail of water on the head, a baby in a shawl on the back, another pail of water in the right hand, and a can of mealies in the left. With the body erect, a swinging, wagging motion of the haunches, the shoulders well squared, the back hollowed, they walk with a firm and regular step, and, as a relief, without removing the long pipe which generally adorns the mouth, they expectorate right and left, describing parabolas fit to make a Tennessee man expire with envy. The Kaffir women are simply beasts of burden.

The habit, contracted in childhood, of carrying heavy weights on the head and walking barefooted, has given these women their decided gait and erectness of body.

The price of a wife is from ten to sixteen oxen. She brings her husband nothing but her virtue, and he asks no other dowry with her. The aim of every native in South Africa is to be rich enough to afford several wives. When he has three, he can knock off work, smoke his pipe, loll in the sunshine, majestically stalk about the kraal, and live in clover generally.

The wife is all the prouder of her husband because he takes things easily and makes her work. She admires him. "Why should he work," said a Kaffir's wife to me one day, "since he is rich enough to have wives to work for him? If I were a man I should do the same." There was resignation and logic in this. Oh, Parisian and American women, who keep men in leading strings, what do you say to this?

Jealousy is not a failing of the South African women, and all these wives live in peace together.

The wife of a Kaffir, a Pondo, a Basuto, or a Zulu, much prefers that her husband should have many wives; first, because it means a sharing of the work to be done, and also because it flatters her pride to think that she belongs to a man who is well-to-do. She is proud of her husband, and puts on her grandest air when she can say, "My husband has many wives."

ZULUS DRINKING BEER. "AS IN ENGLAND, THE LADIES STAND BACK AND LOOK ON."
[*From a Photograph by* H. S. ELLERBECK, *Natal.*]

And she looks down with pity upon the woman who has no companions to share the caresses of her husband.

Good creatures, who understand what is due to the lords of creation!

You should see them going to fetch the beer of the country, and bringing it home on their heads in enormous wide pitchers, and then standing respectfully in line, upright and silent, while the men, squatting in Turkish fashion, drink out of the pitchers. This is gallantry of much the same stamp as Englishmen exhibit when at certain banquets they invite the ladies to look at them from a high gallery.

Here is a family on the road: the man in front, then the wife, followed by the children. I have seen all the inhabitants of a village walking thus: men first, next the women carrying all the loads, after them the children, the whole party in Indian file.

The children are winsome. Where are the children that are not?

I saw, among the different races of South Africa, young girls of from twelve to fifteen, superbly formed, perfect *barbediennes*. Their skin is soft as velvet, their shoulders and arms a sculptor's dream. But, unfortunately, that skin has no elasticity, and early loses its freshness. Married life and motherhood, which so often improve white women, destroy the charms of most of the native women of Africa.

From the European point of view, they are generally ugly in face. However, I saw a pretty one here and there. Among others, I remember a young Kaffir woman who had brought her baby to the doctor of the district to be vaccinated. She had the roguish prettiness of a Parisian woman, and the red kerchief bound about her head and jauntily lifted over one ear, made her quite provokingly picturesque.

When they leave their huts, the Kaffirs, both men and women, wear a blanket dyed with red earth, which, slung over the shoulders, adds much dignity to their

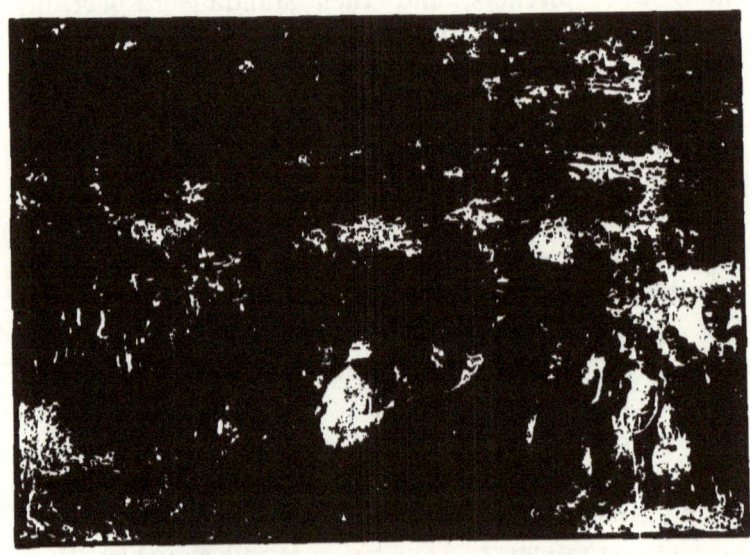

DISTRICT SURGEON VACCINATING ZULUS.
[*From a Photograph by* H. S. ELLERBECK, *Natal.*]

appearance. At home, the men are clothed with the air of the atmosphere, and the women deck themselves with a hundred and one baubles on the neck, arms, and legs. From the wrist to the elbow, the arm is generally covered with a load of brass bangles.

Of all the natives that I saw in South Africa, the Zulus are much the handsomest. What superb fellows those men are! What a happy blending of firmness and gentleness in the look! what dignity in the carriage! Men of over six feet, admirably proportioned, whose movements are simple, dignified, natural, and graceful. Nature has moulded no finer male figures than these. The Zulus are brave, intelligent people, moral and honest; and what helps to keep the race healthy and handsome is, that the men and women never contract very early marriages, while the Kaffirs often marry mere children.

In a kraal a few miles from the spot where the unhappy Prince Imperial met with his sad and untimely death, I saw nine hundred natives of the country, men, women, and children, who had come out of their huts to be examined by the vaccinating doctor. What interesting types there were to study in this assemblage!

The young girls adorn their heads with strings of beads, that hang gracefully about the ears, their necks with more beads, their arms and legs with circlets of brass and beads, and around the waist is a narrow leather belt, from which hangs, in front, an infinitesimal apron of beads and fringe. When they are married, they don a little petticoat about a foot deep. Their hair is greased and brushed straight back off the forehead, in the form of a Turkish fez. The women are generally much smaller than the men, thickset, plump, and shapely in their swarthy beauty.

For the sum of a sovereign, I one day bought the whole costume of a young woman, and carried it off in the side pocket of my coat. After taking off the last piece of adornment, she stood there a few moments smiling, happy, with the money in her hand, as uncon scious of her nudity as a new-born babe, and I looked at her with the same admiration and respect that I should have felt in the presence of a beautiful statue, or of a model with pure sculptural outlines encased in bronze tights.

Among the New Zealand Maoris, the young girl is not virtuous, but once married she is faithful to her husband, who never concerns himself about the life his wife may have led before he married her.

Among the Zulus, the young girl's virtue is exemplary. She may throw everything to the winds, but never her virtue. She may play at love-making, but though she go to the edge of the precipice, she is sure-footed and will never fall. She knows that, so long as she is virtuous, she is worth sixteen oxen to her father, and that if her husband discovered, after marriage, that this was not the case, he would send her back to her father and re-demand his oxen. Her fidelity is a filial one. Her father values her virtue as part of his stock in trade; he tends her, fattens her, and does his best to make her attractive and marketable.

The young woman is proud to feel that she is valuable, and the one who has been sold to her husband for sixteen oxen looks down with contempt upon a member of her sex who has only fetched ten. In Zululand, there are "sets" of the *upper sixteen* who look down on the *lower ten*.

I amused a Kaffir woman very much one day by telling her that, in France, a woman without a dowry very often did not find a husband.

" The women buy their husbands, then, in your country?" she said.

"Yes," I replied, "and sometimes the remnants of a man."

Great was her surprise.

Her reasoning was not so much at fault, after all. She thought that it was more flattering for a woman to be bought by a husband than to have to buy one. Woman has a value in South Africa, she thought. What can her value possibly be in France, where some old notary, who marries a young wife, exacts an indemnity of two hundred thousand francs with her?

A Zulu one day confided to me the following reflections on polygamy in his country:

"It is polygamy, boss, that is the cause of our prosperity. As soon as a Zulu becomes a man, he works hard to save the money to buy a wife. When he has obtained her, and grown tired of her, he sets to work again to earn enough to buy another, and so on."

Old Zulus of patriarchal age go in for matrimony. They are more ambitious and fonder of women than the Kaffirs. Besides, in their hands marriage is a commercial enterprise. These shrewd men buy wives as other people buy live four-footed stock, to increase their wealth. Thus, when the Zulu marries, he hopes to have many daughters, who will be salable and bring him oxen. At the birth of a boy, he makes a wry face.

The Zulus are virtuous, moral, and honest as the day, and the missionaries who have settled there to convert them have gone to the wrong place. If you lose anything, no matter what, in a kraal, and a Zulu finds it, he will run after you. Now, the Zulu can run several miles without stopping, and you may be sure he will not stop until he has overtaken you and handed over that which you left behind. These remarks apply to the Zulu in the raw state. The converted Zulu is quite a different person.

In a hotel at Pietermaritzburg, Natal, I was one day admiring three splendid young Zulus who did chambermaids' and errand boys' work, and I asked the proprietress where she had got them.

"A long way from here," she said, "in a kraal. I never engage natives except in the raw state."

"Why do you not take them," I asked, "from the missionary schools which abound in the neighborhood?"

"Oh," she said, shaking her head, "none of those for me."

This set me thinking. After all, I said to myself, this is only one person's opinion. The proprietress probably has a prejudice against the missionaries. I drew no conclusion, but resolved to put the same question to all the hotel proprietors whom I came across. Everywhere the answer was the same: "No converted Zulus for us."

Many English people will be surprised to hear this, but I can affirm that no one in the Colonies ignores the fact. In the natural state, the Zulus are honest, and their women are virtuous. When they have gone through the apprenticeship of civilization in the missions, the women's virtue often loses much of its rigidity, and the men lie and cheat like "Christians" of the deepest dye.

The Zulus are virtuous and honest *by instinct*, and it is difficult to see how their child-like souls can be improved by a theory which, after all, may be summed up in these few words: "Do not sin, but if you do sin, make yourself easy, you have only to believe and all your sins will be blotted out." "Let us sin, then," say the converted Zulus too often: "the more we sin, the more will be forgiven us." It is not the seed that is bad, it is the ground that is not prepared.

This will not prevent plenty of good English people from continuing to send missionaries to South Africa, nor from making collections to increase their number. I simply state a fact, and give it with the authority of every one who engages native servants in the Cape and in Natal.

Missionaries have never done me any harm, and in this volume I have not to try, thank heaven, to please or displease any one. I say what I think, I repeat what everybody in the Colonies knows, and if, in so doing, I unhappily offend certain people who think they ought to feel offended, I shall sleep none the worse for it.

CHAPTER XXXIV.

The Orange Free State—The Transvaal—A Page or Two of History—The Boers at Home—Manners and Customs—The Boers and the Locusts—The Boers will have to "Mend or End"—Bloemfontein, Pretoria, and Johannesburg.

THE Orange Free State or Boer Republic, and the Transvaal or South African Republic, now independent States, were a few years ago branches of the firm, John Bull & Co.

The Orange Free State is a large desert, five thousand feet above the sea, on a plateau whose superficial area is about equal to that of France. The climate of this country is the driest and healthiest in the world. The land is a succession, a superposition, of plateaus, hills and mountains crowned with enormous boulders. It is desolation, isolation, immensity. Only since seeing the vast landscapes of Africa, have I had a true idea of space.

Towards the middle of this century, a large number of Boers, wishing to escape from the continual encroachments of the English, quitted the Cape, and went with their flocks and herds to an immense district situated between the Vaal and Orange Rivers. They soon organized themselves into a republic, and began to hope that they were now forever out of the reach of the English.

They were mistaken. You are never out of the reach of the English.

The Boers have a bad habit, which has constantly been the cause of quarrels between them and the English. In the eyes of the Boers, the aborigines of South Africa are not human beings to be conciliated, but wild animals to be tracked and exterminated whenever occasion offers. When they did not kill them, they made slaves of them, and drove them to work with great leather whips that they would never have dared used about the oxen that drew their carts. They neither sought to civilize nor instruct them, nor even to convert them, for they do not admit that the negro can have a soul. This did not please the English, who themselves get rid of troublesome natives in the countries which they invade, but get rid of them by a much more diplomatic process—conversion and diversion, the Bible and the bottle.

In 1845 the Boers of the Orange Republic fell upon the Griquas, an important tribe living to the west of them. They were going to exterminate them, when the English came to the rescue of the savages, vanquished the Boers and annexed their territory, under the very plausible pretext that their independence was a continual menace to the tranquillity of South Africa.

A number of Boers, furious at seeing themselves once more under the domination of the English, packed up, crossed the Vaal, and settled in a new country, which they called Transvaal, and where they soon founded a new republic.

A few years later, England, fearing not to be able to control territories that were attaining such alarming proportions, allowed the Boers of the Orange Republic to proclaim afresh their independence (1853), an independence which they still enjoy; but when the diamond mines were discovered in 1870, just where Kimberly now stands, all that district was taken away from the Boers and rechristened British.

The Boers settled in the Transvaal repeated in 1877 the offence which had cost them the independence of the Orange Republic in 1845. They resolved to exterminate the natives of the territory which they had invaded, and were going to put their project into execution when the English conquered and annexed them. Everything seemed lost to them, for it was no use thinking of advancing farther northward. Their only hope was to reconquer their independence, and that at the point of the sword. In 1880 they revolted, and defeated the English at Majuba Hill, after having killed the English general, Sir Pomeroy Colley. The Transvaal was declared free, but under the protection of England, on the 25th of October, 1881. Three years later, England completely retired from the Transvaal.

It is now well known that the Transvaal and the surrounding territories are all underlaid with gold, but it is quite certain that the Boers never will dig for it.* In a very few years the country will be overrun by gold-seekers from all parts of the world. The Boers will continue to scratch the surface of the earth, but they will not dig far below it. They occupy immense

* It is seriously conjectured that it was from these parts that Solomon got the gold for the temple at Jerusalem Searches recently made, proved that a civilization formerly existed in South Africa. I saw in Mr. Cecil Rhodes' study a beautiful bronze statuette which has been excavated in Mashonaland.

tracts of land which they do not cultivate, and in their hands the country makes no progress. I have seen farmers whose farms were as large as Devonshire, and who contented themselves with pasturing cattle on a few hundred acres. They are ignorant, behind the

PROSPECTING FOR GOLD—TRANSVAAL.
[*From a Photograph by* H. S. ELLERBECK, *Natal.*]

times, stubborn, and lazy. They refuse to till the earth with modern implements. They do the kind of farming that was done in the time of Abraham, Isaac, and Jacob. Their houses are often like pigsties. Before going to bed, they take off their boots, and call that undressing. The floor is their bed. Skins are spread on it, and there all the family—men, women, and children—sleep higgledy-piggledy. Once or twice a year they set out in their wagons for the nearest town, where they go through two or three days of devotions. The richest go to the hotels, others erect tents, or live in their wagons during their stay. When they have departed, the inhabitants of the town fumigate the place.

Take all that is dirtiest, bravest, most old-fashioned, and most obstinate in a Breton, all that is most suspicious, sly, and mean in a Norman, all that is shrewdest, most hospitable, and most puritan and bigoted in a Scot, mix well, stir, and serve, and you have a Boer, or if you will—a boor.

No, the world of to-day goes round too rapidly to allow the Boer to stand still. He will have "to mend or end."

For a long time the Boers refused to have trains in the Transvaal, because this kind of locomotion is not mentioned in the Bible, and it was only by calling the railways "steam tramways" that they were induced to have them at all.

The Transvaal Parliament, the Raad, has refused to have the Government Buildings insured against fire, because, "if it be God's will that they shall burn, there is no going against it."

The most sublime thing in this line is the discussion which took place in the Lower House of the Raad on the extermination of locusts (Session 1893).

I have extracted from the papers the following account of part of the debate:

" Dr. Leyds, Secretary of State, read a communication from the Cape and Orange Free State Governments, requesting coöperation in the destruction of locusts.

" Mr. Roos said locusts were a plague, as in the days of King Pharaoh, sent by God ; and the country would assuredly be loaded with shame and obloquy if it tried to raise its hand against the mighty hand of the Almighty.

" Mr. Declerg and Mr. Steenkamp spoke in the same strain, quoting largely from the Scriptures.

" Mr. Wolmarans proposed a general day of prayer and humiliation for South Africa.

" The chairman related a true story of a man whose farm was always spared by the locusts, until one day he caused some to be killed. His farm was devastated.

" Mr. Stoop conjured the members not to constitute themselves terrestrial gods, and oppose the Almighty.

" Mr. Lucas Meyer raised a storm by ridiculing the arguments of the former speakers, and comparing the locusts to beasts of prey, which they destroyed.

" Mr. Labuschagne was violent. He said the locusts were quite different from beasts of prey. They were sacred animals, a special plague sent by God for their sinfulness."

This is how far the Boers have reached in the end of the nineteenth century.

And, in looking at the assembly, you are prepared for anything. A few intelligent heads here and there: but the great majority is composed of rough-looking sons of the soil, with large, square heads, and small, sleepy, though cunning eyes.

The Boers are all dead shots. They do not wildly

aim into the mass; each picks out a man, and that man's hour has come. Every shot tells. If they do aim into the mass, they bring down their enemies thirteen to the dozen. They count on their sure aim to preserve their independence.

The two South African Republics possess three towns

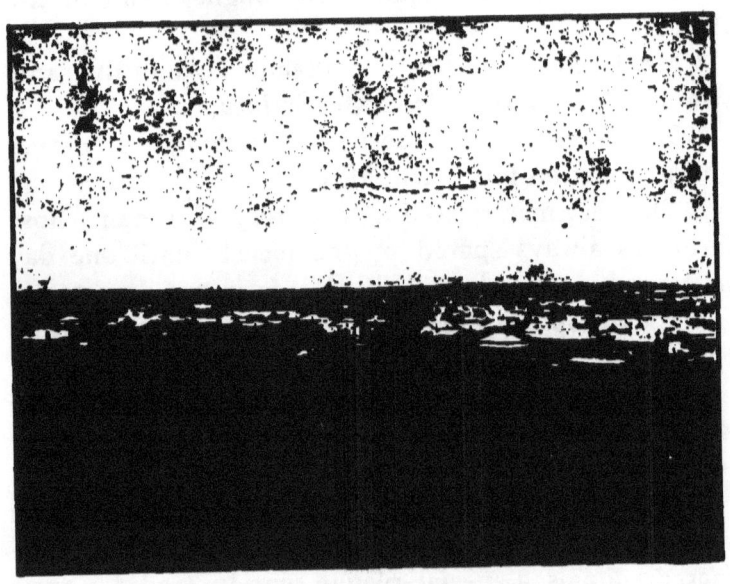

BLOEMFONTEIN, ORANGE FREE STATE.

which must be mentioned: Bloemfontein in the first, Pretoria and Johannesburg in the second.

Bloemfontein is a town of five or six thousand inhabitants, that resembles the most modern towns of the Cape—a market-place, a comfortable club, negroes, dust ankle deep and pure air. The Parliament and the President's house are rather pretty buildings. At one end of the town there is a fort garrisoned by the regular army of the republic, which is composed of about forty soldiers got up like Prussians. But if there are few soldiers in the two republics, every man is brave and a good shot, and twenty thousand men are ready to bear arms in defence of their liberty. Beyond the town, the yellow desert, arid and dusty, stretching away to the horizon.

Pretoria, the capital of the Transvaal, is more interesting. Verdure has been brought there, pretty houses have been built, and the Government Building, which cost over two hundred thousand pounds, is the most massive and imposing-looking public building in South Africa.

As for Johannesburg, that demands a special chapter.

CHAPTER XXXV.

Johannesburg, the Gold City—The Boers again—The Future of the Transvaal—Miraculous Development of Johannesburg—Strange Society—Stranger Wives and Husbands—Aristocracy in Low Water—The Captain and the Magistrate.

THE most marvelous monument of British energy and perseverance is Johannesburg, the city of gold.

Johannesburg, which is seven years old and no more, is to-day a town of 60,000 inhabitants, well built, possessing first-class hotels, shops as important as those of the large European towns, elegant suburbs, dotted over with charming villas; and although there is not a tree to be found growing wild within five hundred miles, Johannesburg has a very promising park and beautiful private gardens. And please to remember that the railway was only brought to Johannesburg a year ago,* so that each stone, each plank, each nail that served to raise this city in the desert, by enchantment, so to speak, must have been brought there in heavy carts drawn by oxen, at the rate of about a mile and a half an hour.

Johannesburg is not only the most important town of the Transvaal, it is the most important town of South Africa.

The Boers cannot boast of having contributed either to its birth or its growth; Johannesburg is a cosmopol-

* At the time I write these lines (December, 1893).

itan town, where every nation seemed to me to be represented except the Transvaal. The Boers are farmers and sportsmen, nothing more. Their ancestors were farmers, and they do not conceive that they themselves could be anything else. Ignorant, bigoted, behind the times, these Dutch Bretons, transplanted in Africa, cultivate the soil like the contemporaries of the patriarchs, and refuse even to look at agricultural machinery. They do not change their ideas—nor their linen. They are hospitable, slaves of routine, dirty, brave, and lazy; they have much religion and few scruples; they are content to live as their ancestors lived, and ready to die on the day that the independence of their country is in danger.

The Transvaal will never be an English colony. The English of the Transvaal, as well as those of Cape Colony and Natal, would be as firmly opposed to it as the Boers themselves, for they have never forgiven England for letting herself be beaten by the Boers at Majuba Hill and accepting her defeat, a proceeding which has rendered them ridiculous in the eyes of the Dutch population of South Africa. Johannesburg will absorb the Transvaal; the apathy of the Boers will be bound to give way to the ever-increasing activity of the English; but the prestige of England will profit nothing by this. The Transvaal is destined to become an Anglo-Saxon republic, which will form part of the United States of South Africa. With me this is not a simple impression, but a firm conviction.

To form an idea of the significance of this town, so flourishing to-day, we must go back to its foundation.

Johannesburg has been raised in the desert. No riv-

JOHANNESBURG,
PAST AND PRESENT.

rivers, no roads, no trees; that is to say, no means of transport, no means of construction. Seven years ago the spot was occupied by a few tents, which served as shelter to the daring pioneers who had ventured thus far to seek for gold, at the risk of death from hunger or at the hands of savages. It was only at the end of two years that they could get enough wood and brick to begin the semblance of a town. The greatest hindrance was the want of water, and those who wished to indulge in the luxury, I do not say of a bath, but a simple ablution, had to do it in seltzer-water at two shillings a bottle. But irrigation works have been carried out, and the town now possesses reservoirs. This is a happy thing, for the price of seltzer-water has not changed. In Johannesburg you pay two shillings for a glass of beer, one and sixpence for a cigar, and everything else is proportionately expensive; but the inhabitants earn money easily, and so no one grumbles.

The streets of Johannesburg are wide and straight; the town possesses pretty theatres, excellent hotels, and, I repeat, all that modern civilization can demand.

Experts assure us that the gold mines of Johannesburg are inexhaustible. If this be true, and I do not doubt it, in less than ten years this town will be one of the largest commercial centres of the world.

At present it is a gambling den, where you are blinded by dust, but need strictly to keep your eyes open. Alongside distinguished, serious, and most honorable people, you have a decidedly mixed and contraband society—millionaires, broken-down swells, shoddy barons, and financial gamblers, adventurers of all nations—German, English, French, Italian, Greek, Levantine, Jews, by birth and by profession, living from hand to mouth, passing their lives between the hope of being millionaires and the fear of being bankrupt. Pretty women, with painted cheeks and tinted hair, on the lookout for adventures, dying of ennui, passing their lives in card-playing, dining and dancing; while the men are at the Stock Exchange, the club, or drinking and chatting with barmaids covered in rouge and diamonds, and whose wages are twenty-five pounds a month without extras. Dwelling in the midst of these, I repeat, exists a colony of delightful people, who necessarily hold somewhat aloof from this crowd—an aristocracy of manners, a choice set, composed of financiers, merchants, engineers, people such as one meets in the best society in Europe, and of whom I have not spoken much, precisely because they differ in nothing from their fellows in any other community.

Well, after all, the history of Johannesburg is but the history of San Francisco, Denver, and every other town in the world to which the discovery of a precious metal has suddenly attracted an adventurous population in search of easy gains. Towns of this kind, and the most flourishing of them, are like revolutions—they have been started by adventurers. I do not by any means employ the word *adventurer* in its objectionable sense.

What strange ups and downs they see, some of these adventurers! What cases of pluck, and what pocketing of pride you meet with, and cannot but admire!

In an Australasian town I visited, there was at the hotel an Englishman of high breeding, good education, and perfect manners, filling the position of handy-man. He kept the accounts, watered the garden, wielded a feather-duster on occasions, and went to the quay to meet the boats and secure patronage for the establishment, wearing a cap bearing the name of the hotel in red letters. This man had been a captain in the English army; he was an officer no longer, but still every inch a gentleman.

I remember an English lord who was philosophically earning his bread by making jam-tarts in a Californian town. The baker who employed him paid him a dollar a day. He accepted his position without much murmuring; but he had one thing to complain of, which was that the Chinese cooks in California worked so cheaply that this occupation seemed to hold out no prospect of future advancement. "These confounded Chinamen," he would exclaim; "if it was not for them, one could get on!"

What pathos in these few words!

In its own line, the following incident is still more piquant:

At the Cape I had made the acquaintance of an Englishman, well informed, well dressed, full of good spirits, excellent company, a man holding a good position in the town. I met with him again at the club of an inland town. My manager and I were talking to him when another gentleman came into the smoking-room, took up a paper, and sat near by to read it.

"Ah," said our Englishman, "there is my old friend Brown; I must introduce you. He is one of the magistrates of the town, a charming fellow; he will be delighted to know you."

Gay as a lark, light as a feather, he rose, went to fetch his friend, brought him to us, and made the introduction.

"My old friend Brown," said he, tapping him lightly on the shoulder.

Mr. Brown bowed rather stiffly, exchanged a few words with us, and reapplied himself to his newspaper.

Our Englishman left us. We remained in the smoking-room. Mr. Brown, in the friendliest manner possible, came back to us.

"What impudence," he began, "to introduce me to you as one of his old friends! In my capacity of magistrate, I gave him three years' imprisonment for embezzlement five years ago."

"My old friend Brown! a charming fellow!" I thought the thing was immensely droll.

CHAPTER XXXVI.

"Oom" Paul, President of the Transvaal—John Bull's Redoubtable Adversary—A Short Interview with this Interesting Personage—A Picturesque Meeting between two Diplomats.

MR. PAUL KRÜGER, President of the Transvaal, is a man whose personality is one of the most striking in South Africa. One may say that on the figures of President Krüger and Mr. Cecil Rhodes all the political interest of the country is centered. Mr. Cecil Rhodes, the pioneer of British civilization, alert and enterprising; President Krüger, the old Boer, cautious, slow-going, patriotic, the last defender of Dutch interests, a wily diplomat, who, the head of a little republic composed of about twenty thousand men able to bear arms, holds his own against the British, has foiled them more than once by diplomacy, and once beaten them in battle on Majuba Hill. Mr. Cecil Rhodes, who drives the wheels of the South African chariot; "Oom" Paul, who acts as a drag on these wheels.

His Honor, the President of the South African Republic, or of the Transvaal, surnamed by his people "*Oom Paul*" (Uncle Paul), is a thick-set man, rather below the middle height, who carries his seventy-odd years lightly. His forehead is narrow, his nose and mouth large and wide, his eyes small and blinking, like those of a forest animal; his voice so gruff and sonorous, that his *ya* is almost a roar. From his left hand the thumb is wanting. It was he himself, when a child, who, having one day hurt this thumb badly, took it clean off with a blow from a hatchet. He barely knows how to write, and he speaks in that primitive language, the Dutch patois spoken by the South African farmers:

"OOM" PAUL, PRESIDENT OF THE TRANSVAAL.

I is, thou is, he is; We is, you is, they is. Uncle Paul's eye is half veiled, but always on the lookout: it is the eye that he is obliged to keep on the English. The wily one says he does not speak nor understand a word of English. I am willing to believe it, although the joke is hard to assimilate.

I had the pleasure of being introduced to "Oom" Paul by Monsieur Aubert, French consul in the Transvaal. It was in the Parliament, or Raad, during the few minutes' interval allowed to the President and members for a smoke between the debates. I begged him to

"OOM" PAUL'S PRIVATE RESIDENCE, PRETORIA.

give me a few moments' interview in his own house, and he willingly made an appointment for five o'clock that evening. The editor of the *Pretoria Press* very kindly accompanied me, and acted as interpreter.

I do not know if President Krüger took me for some spy in the pay of the English, but I seemed to inspire him with little confidence, and during the twenty minutes that the interview lasted he never looked me once in the face. Whenever I asked him a question, he took some time to think over his answer; and then it would come out in a weighty manner, the words uttered slowly, having been turned over at least seven times in his mouth. Here, in a few words, is the gist of the conversation:

"I suppose, Mr. President, that since the victory that your brave little nation gained over the English on Majuba Hill, the Boers bear no animosity to England?"

"To-morrow is the 24th of May, and, in honor of Queen Victoria's birthday, I have adjourned the Parliament."

Here, to begin with, was a response which for caution I thought worthy of a Scot.

"They fear in England," I went on, "that the victory may have made you arrogant."

"That is absurd; the English might easily have repaired their defeat and crushed us. They recoiled at the idea of annihilating a people who had shown that they were ready to shed the last drop of their blood to save their independence."

"Johannesburg is, I see, completely given over to the English. Before ten years have passed, the gold mines will have attracted to the Transvaal a British population greatly outnumbering the Boers. And Johannesburg is hardly forty miles from your capital."

"The English are welcome in Johannesburg. They help us to develop the resources of the Transvaal, and in nowise threaten the independence of the country."

"That is true, Mr. President; but the Transvaal seems to be now surrounded on all sides. I hear of troubles in Matabeleland, and if the English take possession of that vast territory* you will be completely encircled."

"That is why I claim Swaziland, which will allow us to extend our country towards the sea."

"Towards the sea, yes; but to the sea, no."

"I can count upon eighteen thousand men, sir, who will die to the last man to defend the independence of their country."

And the only reply that I could obtain to one or two more questions on the dangerous position of the republic which he governs, may be summed up in these words: "We are ready to die, every one of us."

But they will not need to die; for if ever the English invaded the Transvaal in their search for gold, and succeeded in getting the government of it into their own hands, they would keep it an independent republic; that is to say, they would take into their own hands the reins now held by "Oom" Paul, and the change would only be a change of coachmen. The English Crown will not profit by the change, for the Transvaal, I repeat it, will never be an English colony again.

The President's mode of life is primitive. He smokes an enormous pipe in the drawing-room, where our interview takes place, and expectorates on the carpet in the most unceremonious manner. His salary is £8,000 a year, and his indemnity for public expenses £500 a year. He saves the salary, and lives comfortably on the indemnity.

When it was decided that Sir Henry Loch, High Commissioner for South Africa, and President Krüger should meet and discuss the details of the Swaziland

* They have taken possession of it since this interview.

Convention, they both journeyed to Colesberg, and both put up at the same hotel.

It is President Krüger's habit to rise at five every morning.

Having taken a night's rest after his journey, Sir Henry Loch rose at six to take his morning tub.

On his way to the bathroom, in the usual light costume, he passed in the corridor the quaint figure of "Oom" Paul, enjoying his early smoke, in a frock coat covered with orders, a high hat, and—slippers.

Opposite his house stands a church where the Doppers of Pretoria assemble on Sundays. It is often "Oom" Paul who preaches the sermon. He loves theological discussions. He is a mixture of the Scot and the Norman. Even this mixture fails to give an idea of the shrewd and clever Dopper.

CHAPTER XXXVII.

The Success of the Firm, John Bull & Co. — The Explanation—The Freest Countries of the World—Illustrations to Prove it—The Future of the British Empire—Reflections of a Sour Critic—Advice to Young Men—And Now Let Us Go and Look on an Old Wall Covered with Ivy.

It is neither by his intelligence nor by his talents that John Bull has built up that British Empire, of which this little volume can give the reader but a faint idea; it is by the force of his character.

Thomas Carlyle calls the English "of all the Nations in the World the stupidest in speech," but he also rightly calls them "the wisest in action." It is true that John Bull is slow to conceive; but when he has taken a resolution there is no obstacle that will prevent his putting it into execution. There are three qualities that guarantee success to those who possess them. John Bull has them all three: an audacity that allows him to undertake any enterprise, a dogged perseverance that makes him carry it through, and a philosophy that makes him look upon any little defeats he may now and then meet with as so many moral victories that he has won. He never owns himself beaten, never doubts of the final success of his enterprise; and is not a battle half won when one is sure of gaining the victory?

To keep up the British Empire, an empire of more than four hundred million souls, scattered all over the globe, to add to its size day by day by diplomacy, by a discreetness which hides all the machinery of government, without functionaries, with a handful of soldiers and more often mere volunteers, is it anything short of marvelous? And at this hour, I guarantee that not one single colony causes John Bull the least apprehension.

One magistrate and a dozen policemen administer and keep in order districts as large as five or six departments of France. There is the same justice for the natives as for the colonists. No Lynch law, as in America. The native, accused of the most atrocious crime, gets a fair trial, and a proper jury decides whether he is innocent or guilty.

All those young nationalities, Canada, Australia, New Zealand, and South Africa, enjoy the most complete liberty, political and social. The English respect their susceptibilities so much, that during the Transvaal War, the Cape Parliament having decided to refuse to allow the English troops to disembark at Cape Town, General Roberts and his army were obliged to land at Durban, and arrived too late to save General Colley, who was killed at Majuba Hill, or to prevent the destruction of his men. John Bull did not consider himself more at home at the Cape on this occasion than a father visiting his son-in-law would consider himself in his own house.

During my stay in Africa a company of musicians announced a concert at Bloemfontein, the Boer capital. According to the English custom, the program was to terminate with "God save the Queen."

It was a want of tact on the part of the artistes, no doubt.

The authorities ordered that the English national anthem should be taken out of the program.

If, in any part of the British Empire, any singer took it into his head to sing "God save the President of the Boer Republic," I guarantee that there would be no objection raised to it. On the contrary, the English would probably say, "Why, that is a song quite new to us, let us go to hear it."

The Chief-Justice, the first magistrate of the colony of Victoria in 1892, was a republican, a partisan of Australian autonomy. He hid his opinions from no one: but his talents as a jurisconsult and his reputation as a man of integrity were so well known and appreciated, that John Bull did not hesitate an instant about placing him at the head of the colonial bench.

All these new countries, which are so many outlets for the commerce of the world, are not monopolized by the English for their own use only. People from other nations may go there and settle without having any formality to go through, or any foreign tax to pay. They may go on speaking their own language, practicing their own religion, and may enjoy every right of citizenship. And if they are not too stubborn or too old to learn, they may lay to heart many good lessons in those nurseries of liberty.

If I have not succeeded in proving that, in spite of their hundred and one foibles, the Anglo-Saxons are the only people on this earth who enjoy perfect liberty, I have lost my time, and I have made you lose yours, dear reader.

The inhabitants of the Colonies in the present day

are proud to call themselves Australians, Canadians, and Afrikanders. The spirit of nationality grows stronger day by day, and it is John Bull himself who feeds it. Every Englishman who goes and settles in the Colonies, ceases after a few years to be English; he is a Canadian, an Australian, or an Afrikander, and swears by his new country. These Anglo-Saxons have an aptitude, a genius, for government inborn in them, and it is out of pure politeness toward the old mother-country that they accept the Governors she sends them, and this only on the understood condition that they shall occupy themselves as little about politics as do the Queen and members of the Royal Family. If the Queen of England dared to say in public that she preferred Conservatives to Liberals, the English monarchy would not have ten years to live. If the Governor of any colony allowed himself to speak on politics in public, except by the mouth of ministers elected by the people, that colony would proclaim its independence the week after, and the Governor would have to avail himself of the first steamer sailing for England.

If ever any colony mentioned in this volume should proclaim her independence, she may gain prestige in her own eyes, but she will not be casting off any yoke, for she could not be freer than she is at present. She will be a junior partner starting business on her own account, and thenceforth dispensing with the help of the head of the firm, who guided her early steps without ever demanding an account of her movements.

There are many people in England who believe that the future fate of the British Empire is to be a Confederation, having London for its centre, and that the

Colonies will favor the scheme. If there is one profound conviction that I have acquired in all my travels among the Anglo-Saxons in the different parts of the world, it is that the Colonies do not want confederation, and will never move toward the realization of this dream in which so many patriotic Britons indulge. To begin with, the Colonies are much too jealous of one another to care for amalgamation. Each one will insist on keeping its individuality, nay, its nationality. Moreover, not one of them has the least desire to be mixed up in any quarrels that England may one day have with any European power. John Bull would be wise to get the confederation idea out of his head. With the exception of Canada, which may possibly one day become part of the United States, the Colonies will remain branches of the firm, John Bull & Co., or they will become independent. For any one who has felt the pulse of those countries, it is impossible to think otherwise.

A sour and unkind critic might thus sum up his impressions of the British Colonies in the southern hemisphere: "I have seen mountains without trees (South Africa), trees without shade (Australia), plains without herbage, rivers without water, flowers without perfume, birds without songs, a sun without pity, dust without mercy, towns without interest," etc.

A kinder and fairer critic would reply to this assertion: "It is certain that the countries which have a future are less interesting to the traveler with artistic tastes than the countries which have a long history. America and the Colonies have no old cathedrals nor ruined castles to show. The inhabitants of the Colonies are enterprising people, who in half a century have founded cities, I might say nations, capable of competing in commercial importance with cities and nations that it has taken ten centuries to develop. I have seen in the Colonies, skies without clouds, winters without cold, festivity without boredom, food almost without cost, hospitality without calculation, millionaires without pride, birds with gorgeous plumage, trees with health-giving properties (how such a list could be extended!), and kind hearts everywhere."

There are two kinds of critics, those who complain that roses have thorns, others who are grateful that thorns have roses.

The colonials have all the qualities and all the little foibles of the English, and if isolation has intensified some of their faults, it has also accentuated their virtues.

For any young man, steady, hard-working, and persevering, no country offers such present advantages and future chances as the Colonies.

The Colonies have no room for *blasé* young Europeans who have only the remnants of themselves to offer. They are like fair young brides with the consciousness of their own worth; what they want is fresh and ardent youth, workers of all sorts, skilled artisans, intelligent vineyard hands, hardy field laborers, men with healthy bodies and upright minds, practical and laborious, To all such the Colonies promise success, and invariably keep their word.

If I were a young man of twenty, I would probably

go and settle in one of these young countries, but I have arrived at an age when it is hardly possible for a man to start a new life. I am too much attached by a life's souvenirs to old Europe to be able now to do without her.

After years of travels through new countries, I was longing to see some old ruin that would remind me that the world had other pages than these freshly written ones.

The day before I left South Africa to return to Europe, Sir Thomas Upington, the genial and witty judge of Cape Town, said to me :

" Well, after all these long travels, what are you going to do now ? "

" What am I going to do ? " I replied. " I am going to Europe to look at some old wall with a bit of ivy on it."

www.ingramcontent.com/pod-product-compliance
Lightning Source LLC
Chambersburg PA
CBHW030747230426
43667CB00007B/870